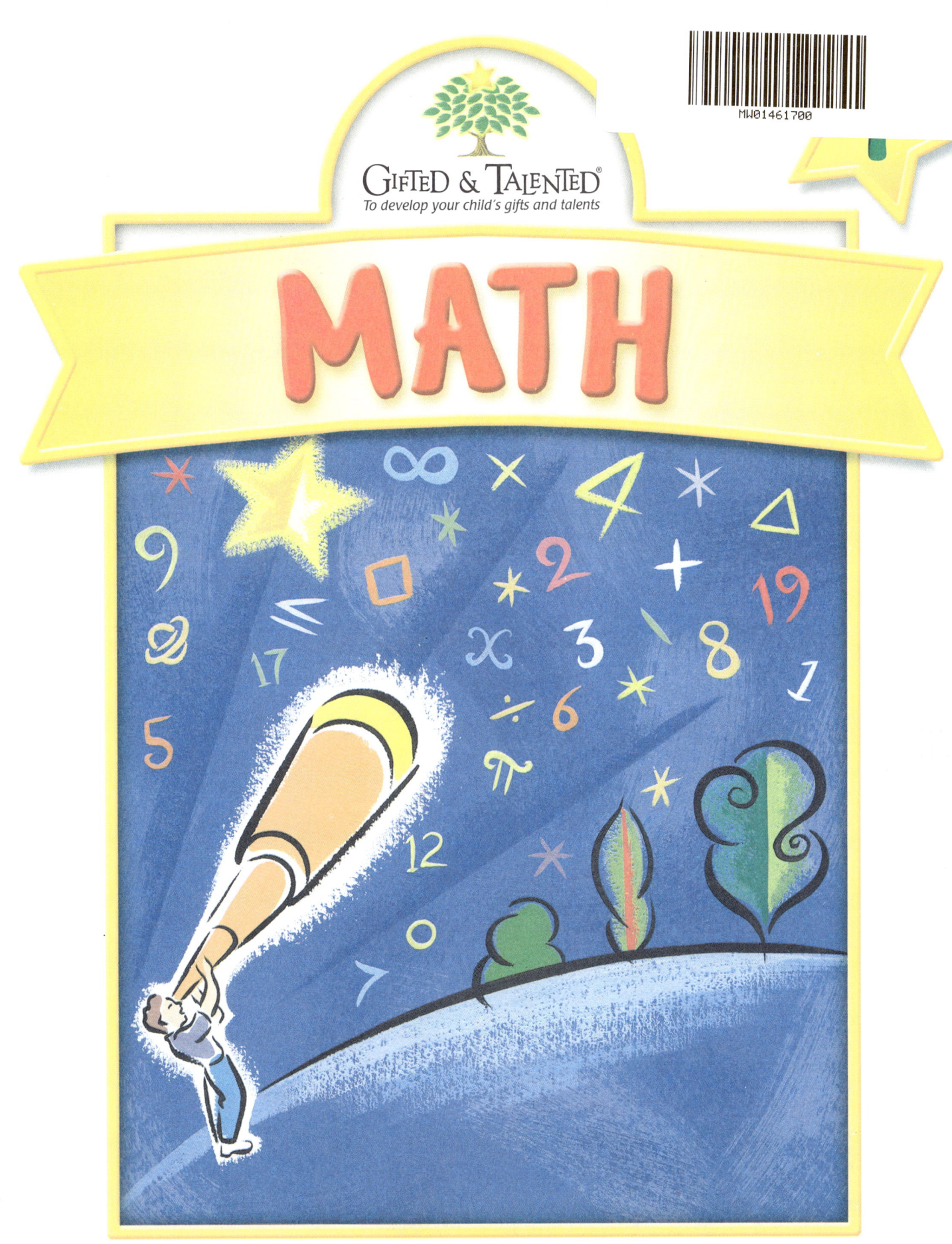

GIFTED & TALENTED®
To develop your child's gifts and talents

MATH

Written by Vicky Shiotsu

McGraw Hill Children's Publishing
Columbus, Ohio

Dear Parents,

Gifted & Talented Math has been designed specifically to promote the development of critical and creative thinking skills. The activities in this book include visual puzzles, logic problems, riddles, and more. All of the activities will spark your child's imagination, sharpen thinking skills, and foster a love of learning.

The activities in this book have been organized according to topics and skills outlined in current math standards. They are intended to reinforce and extend the math concepts your child has already been introduced to at school or at home. For example, in the section on operations and computation, your child will need to apply the concepts of addition and subtraction to solve a variety of challenging problems.

Some of the activities have been grouped so that they give your child practice using a certain type of thinking strategy. For example, two logic problems may be placed side by side so that when your child figures out how to solve the first one, he or she may apply those skills to solve the second one. Each problem, however, can stand alone and does not have to be done in any particular order.

Most of the problems can be completed directly on the workbook pages. In some instances, though, your child might prefer to use a separate sheet of paper to figure out the answers. For certain pages, suggestions are given for using coins and other manipulatives to help your child solve the problems.

While working in this book, your child may be inspired by the activities to create his or her own problems. If so, have your child present the problems to you and explain the answers. Praise your child's efforts and encourage him or her to continue making more problems and puzzles. This type of activity not only stimulates creativity, but it also deepens your child's understanding of mathematical concepts and increases the ability to reason mathematically.

McGraw Hill Children's Publishing

Copyright © 2003 McGraw-Hill Children's Publishing.

Printed in the United States of America. All rights reserved. Except as permitted under the United States Copyright Act, no part of this publication may be reproduced or distributed in any form or by any means, or stored in a database or retrieval system, without prior written permission from the publisher, unless otherwise indicated.

Send all inquiries to:
McGraw-Hill Children's Publishing
8787 Orion Place
Columbus, OH 43240-4027

ISBN 1-57768-941-0

1 2 3 4 5 6 7 8 9 10 VHG 07 06 05 04 03 02

The McGraw·Hill Companies

Table of Contents

Number Sense
Spilled Numbers 5
Order, Order! 6
On the Road 7
Who's Who? 8
Mouse and Cheese 9
Flying Home 10
Cooking Up Numbers 11
Mystery Numbers 12-13

Operations and Computations
What's in the Hat? 14
Make Them Equal 15
Find and Circle 16
Sums to 12 17
Juggling Fun 18
High-Flying Numbers 19
Party Time 20

Patterns
Frankie Frog 21
All Aboard! 22
Caterpillar Patterns 23
Dots and Lines 24
Shape Patterns 25

Money
Piggy Bank Riddles 26
Make 25 Cents 27
Coin Patterns 28
A Toy Sale 29
At the Balloon Shop 30

Logical Thinking
A Flower Garden 31
Toy Bunnies 32
Four Dinosaurs 33

Four Brothers 34
Taking a Trip 35
Eager Beaver 36
Sorting Shapes 37
Circus Fun 38
Which Clown? 39
Roger's Triangles 40
How Many Cookies? 41
Library Lineup 42

Measurement
To the Doghouse 43
Paper Caterpillars 44
Heavier or Lighter? 45
Ounces or Pounds? 46
How Much Time Does It Take? 47

Geometry
Shape Puzzles 48
Shape Designs 49
Hidden Squares 50
How Many Triangles? 51
Paper Cutouts 52
Shape Search 53
Robot Riddles 54
What's on the Bottom? 55
Color and Count 56

Statistics and Probability
Cool Scoops 57
Benny's Outfits 58
Jenny's Outfits 59
Goldfish Pets 60

Answer Key 61-64

Spilled Numbers

Name _____

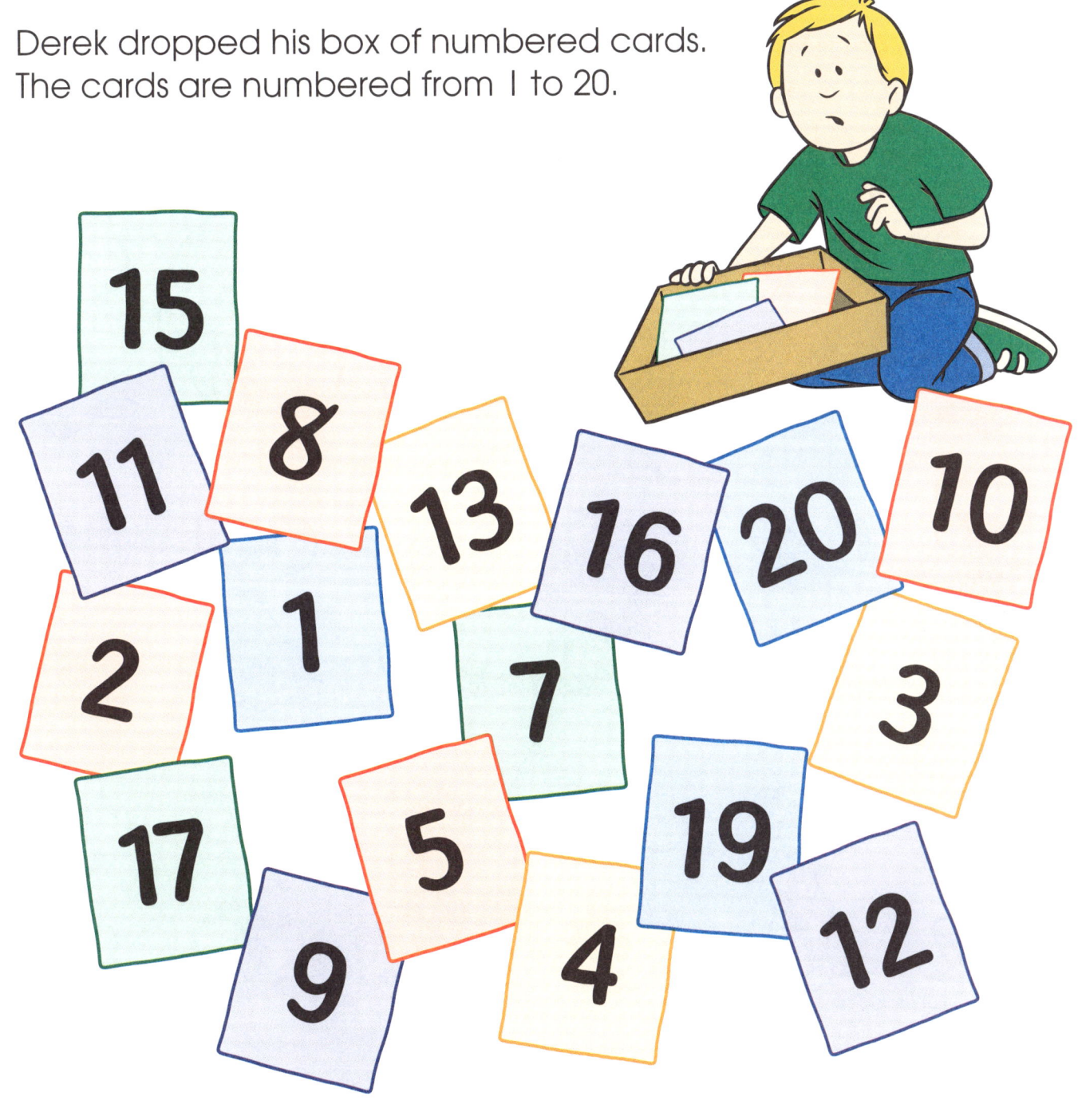

Derek dropped his box of numbered cards. The cards are numbered from 1 to 20.

Look at the numbers carefully. There are three cards still left in the box.

Which numbers are they? _____

Order, Order!

Name _____

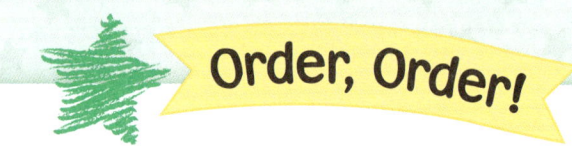

The mice in each row are to line up in order according to their numbers, from smallest to largest. But some mice are not in the right place. In each row, circle the mouse that is out of order. Draw an arrow to show where that mouse should go.

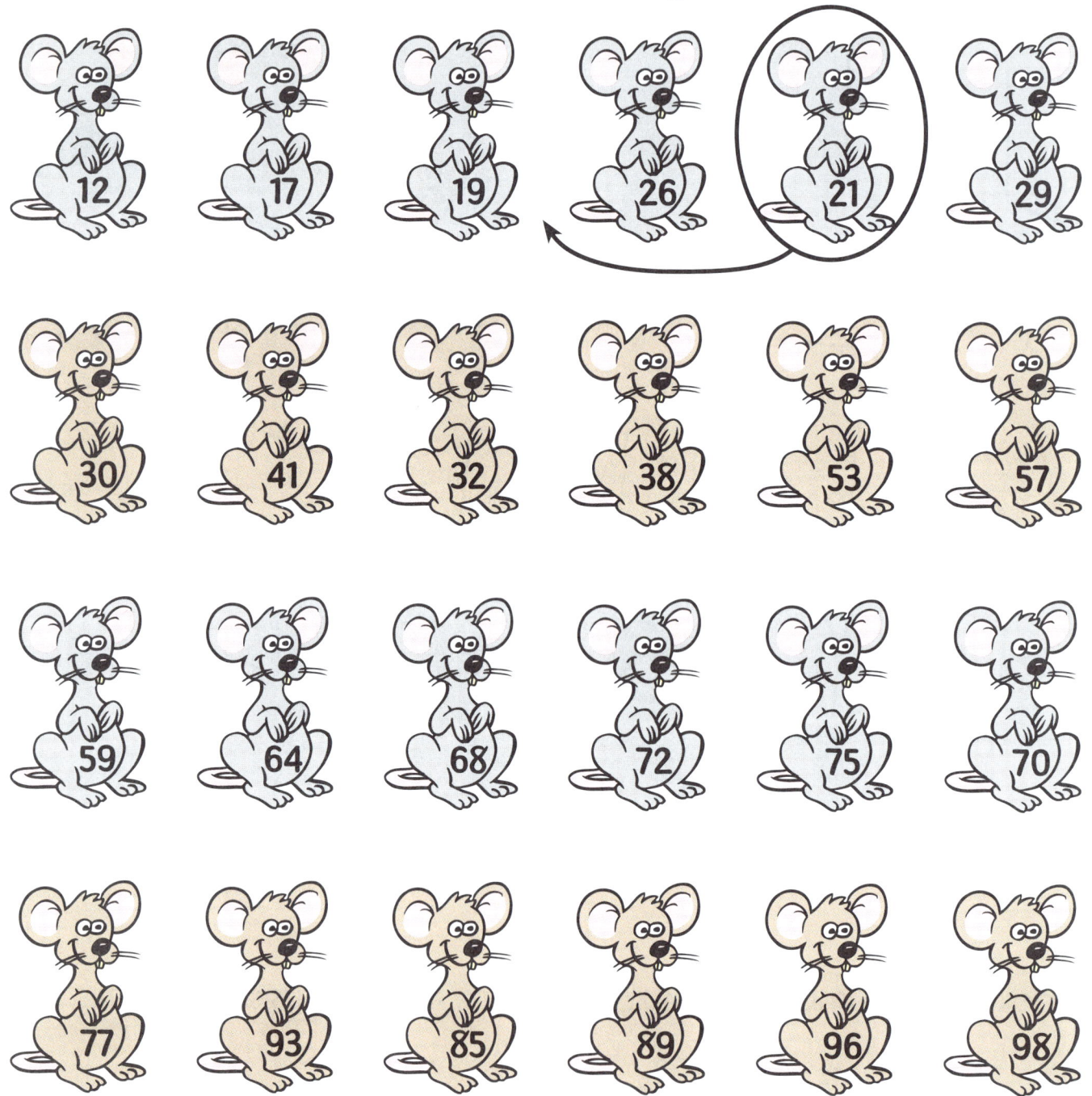

Row 1: 12, 17, 19, 26, 21, 29

Row 2: 30, 41, 32, 38, 53, 57

Row 3: 59, 64, 68, 72, 75, 70

Row 4: 77, 93, 85, 89, 96, 98

Gifted & Talented Math Grade 1 — Number Sense

On the Road

Name _____

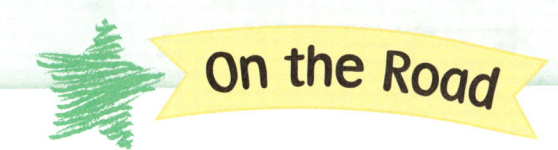

These cars are supposed to be traveling in order, from the largest to the smallest number. But some cars are not in the right place. In each row, circle the car that is out of order. Draw an arrow to show where that car should go.

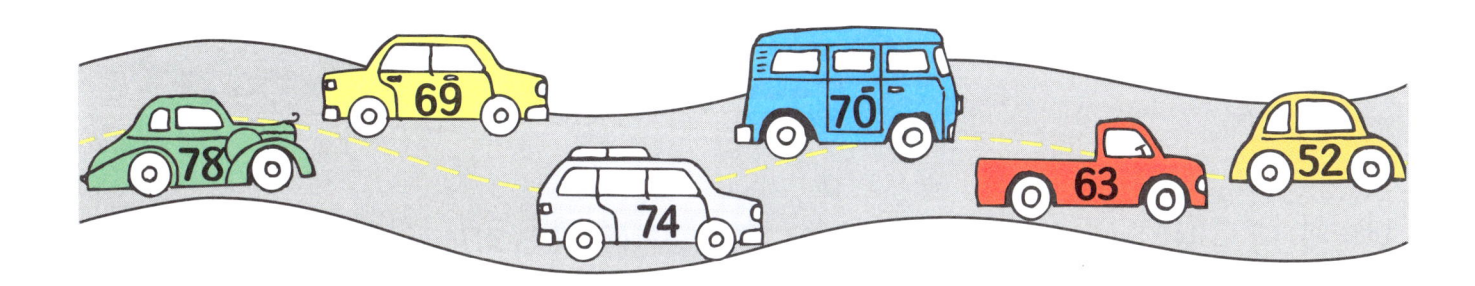

Gifted & Talented Math Grade 1   7   Number Sense

Who's Who?

Name _____

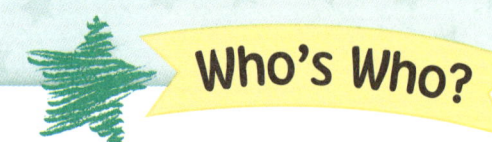

Todd — I'm 7.
Abby — I'm 11.
Becky — I'm 10.
Joni — I'm 9.
Eric — I'm 8.
Ryan — I'm 12.

Use the clues to help you write the correct names on the lines.

1. I am younger than all of the girls. I am not the youngest.

   Who am I? _____

2. I am older than Eric. I am younger than Becky.

   Who am I? _____

3. I am older than two of the girls. I am not a boy.

   Who am I? _____

4. I am not a girl. I am older than Abby.

   Who am I? _____

5. I am a boy. I am five years younger than the oldest boy.

   Who am I? _____

6. I am younger than Abby. I am older than Joni.

   Who am I? _____

Gifted & Talented Math Grade 1 — Number Sense

Mouse and Cheese

Name _____

An even number ends in 2, 4, 6, 8, or 0. Look at the numbers below. Help the mouse get to the cheese by coloring a path of even numbers.

12	24	6	3
7	11	5	14	21
18	26	10	2	15
4	13	1	19	17
8	22	16	20

Write the even numbers on the path in order from smallest to largest.

_____

_____

Gifted & Talented Math Grade 1   Number Sense

Flying Home

Name _____

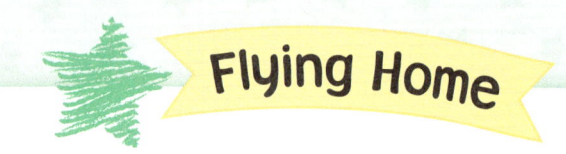

An odd number ends in 1, 3, 5, 7, or 9. Help the bee get to its home by coloring a path of odd numbered flowers.

15	9	13	7
28	16	4	12	21
30	43	39	37	25
50	51	44	32	40
20	49	36	54	60
24	23	35	47

Which number on the path is the largest odd number? _____

Gifted & Talented Math Grade 1   10   Number Sense

Cooking Up Numbers

Name _____

Look at the numbers in the bowls below. Use them to write numbers that match the clues. For each set of clues, do not use a number in a bowl more than once.

1. The number is even. It is greater than 30. It is less than 35.

   Bowl: 1, 2, 3, 6

   _____

2. The number is odd. It is greater than 50. It is less than 60.

   Bowl: 4, 7, 5, 8

   _____

3. The number is even. It is greater than 60. It is less than 70.

   Bowl: 6, 9, 4, 3

   _____

4. The number is odd. It is greater than 25. It is less than 40.

   Bowl: 4, 7, 2, 1

   _____

5. The number is even. It is greater than 70. It is less than 90.

   Bowl: 3, 8, 6, 5

   _____

6. The number is odd. It is greater than 75. It is less than 85.

   Bowl: 9, 2, 3, 7

   _____

7. The number is even. It is greater than 80. It is less than 90.

   Bowl: 7, 8, 2, 1

   _____

Gifted & Talented Math Grade 1 — Number Sense

Mystery Numbers

Name _____

Read each set of clues. Figure out the mystery numbers. Then write them on the lines.

1. The number is odd.

   The number is more than 9.

   The number is less than 13.

   The mystery number is _____.

2. The number is even.

   The number is more than 8 + 8.

   The number is less than 10 + 10.

   The mystery number is _____.

Gifted & Talented Math Grade 1   Number Sense

Name _____

3. The number is more than 50.

   The number is less than 70.

   Count by tens, and you say the number.

   The mystery number is _____.

4. The number is more than 30.

   The number is less than 40.

   Count by fives, and you say the number.

   The mystery number is _____.

Make up your own clues for a mystery number.
Ask a friend or family member to figure out the mystery number.

_____

_____

_____

_____

What's in the Hat?

Name _____

Michael the Magician has a great trick. He pulls bunnies out of his hat! Read each clue. Count the bunnies you see. Then write how many bunnies are hiding in Michael's hat.

1. There are 7 bunnies in all.

   How many are in the hat? ____

2. There are 10 bunnies in all.

   How many are in the hat? ____

3. There are 12 bunnies in all.

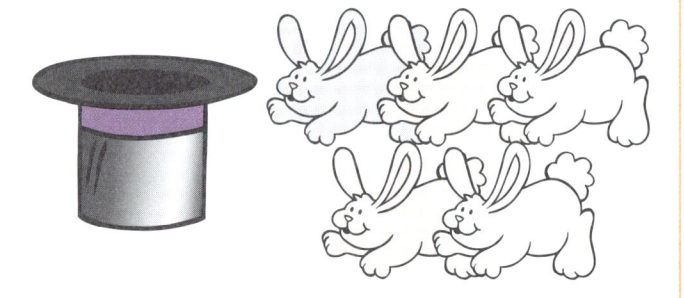

   How many are in the hat? ____

4. There are 9 bunnies in all.

   How many are in the hat? ____

5. There are 14 bunnies in all.

   How many are in the hat? ____

6. There are 15 bunnies in all.

   How many are in the hat? ____

Gifted & Talented Math Grade 1   Operations and Computations

Make Them Equal

Name _____

Look at the numbers in each row. Write **+** or **−** in the circles to make two number sentences that are equal.

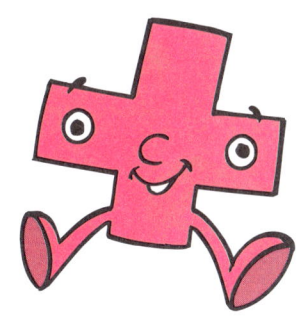

1. 6 ⊕ 3 = 11 ⊖ 2

2. 5 ◯ 2 = 10 ◯ 7

3. 6 ◯ 2 = 12 ◯ 4

4. 8 ◯ 6 = 9 ◯ 5

5. 12 ◯ 3 = 17 ◯ 8

6. 16 ◯ 8 = 5 ◯ 3

7. 9 ◯ 6 = 8 ◯ 7

8. 11 ◯ 3 = 17 ◯ 9

Find and Circle

Name _____

Look at the numbers in the box. Circle three numbers that add up to 10. The numbers can go across or down. Keep going until you have found all the sets. When you are done, all the numbers in the box should be circled.

3	2	6	1	3
2	8	5	4	1
5	0	9	0	1
4	4	2	2	2
7	3	0	2	7
1	8	1	6	1

Gifted & Talented Math Grade 1

Operations and Computations

Sums to 12

Name _____

Use the numbers 1 to 9. Find three different numbers that add up to 12. Write them in the boxes below. See if you can make four number sentences. (You cannot use a number more than once in each sentence.)

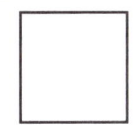

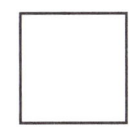

[5] + [1] + [6] = 12

[6] + [0] + [6] = 12

[ ] + [ ] + [ ] = 12

[ ] + [ ] + [ ] = 12

Now write number sentences with four numbers that add up to 12.

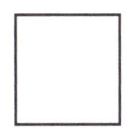

[ ] + [ ] + [ ] + [ ] = 12

[ ] + [ ] + [ ] + [ ] = 12

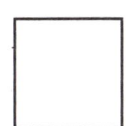

Juggling Fun

Name _____

Write the numbers 1 to 9 on the juggling balls. Use each number only once. The sum of the three numbers on each cat's juggling balls must match the number on that cat's tag.

Gifted & Talented Math Grade 1

18

Operations and Computations

High-Flying Numbers

Write the numbers 1 to 9 in the three sections of the hot-air balloons. The three numbers on each balloon must add up to 15. Use each number only once. Cross off the numbers on the cloud as you use them. Three of the numbers have been filled in for you.

~~1~~ ~~2~~ ~~3~~
4   5   6
7   8   9

1

2

3

Gifted & Talented Math Grade 1

Operations and Computations

Party Time

Name _____

Solve these problems.

1. There are 8 children at a birthday party. There is the same number of boys and girls.

   How many children are boys? _____

   How many children are girls? _____

2. There are 12 balloons. For every red balloon, there are 2 yellow balloons.

   How many balloons are red? _____

   How many balloons are yellow? _____

3. There are 8 presents at the party. Some presents are in boxes and some are in bags. There are 4 more boxes than bags.

   How many boxes are there? _____

   How many bags are there? _____

Gifted & Talented Math Grade 1 Operations and Computations

Frankie Frog

Name _____

Frankie Frog loves to jump! He also loves to jump and make patterns. Look at the number lines below. Figure out the patterns. For each pattern, write the next number that Frankie will land on.

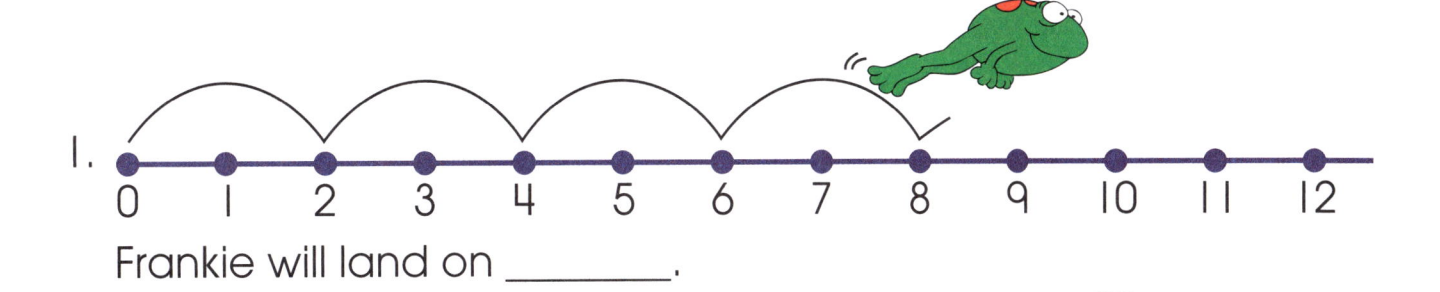

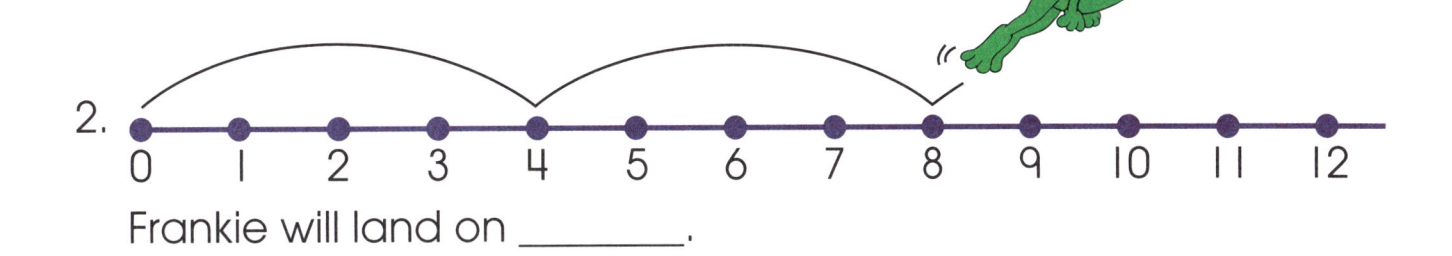

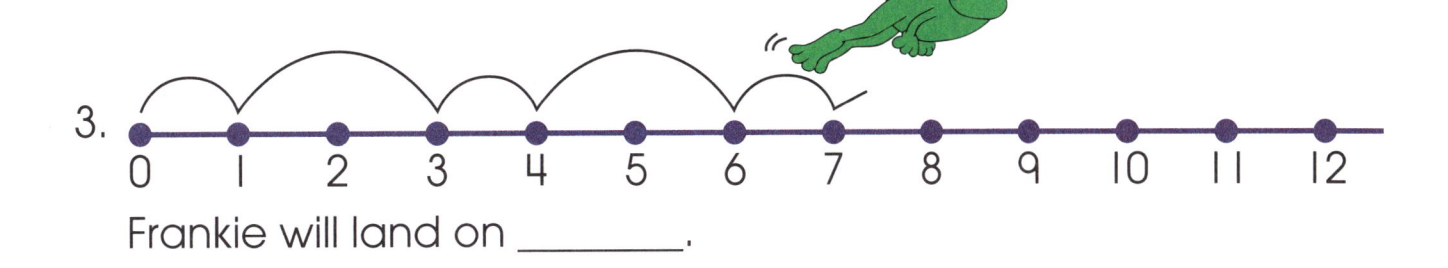

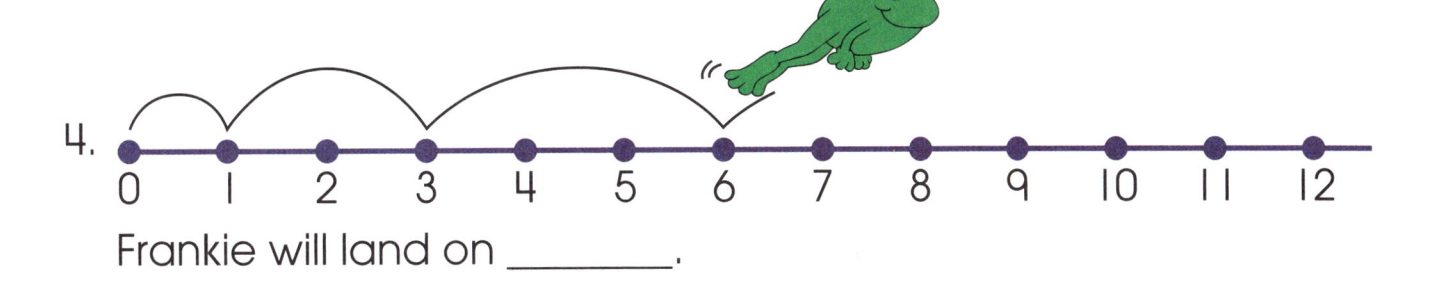

1. Frankie will land on _____.

2. Frankie will land on _____.

3. Frankie will land on _____.

4. Frankie will land on _____.

Gifted & Talented Math Grade 1 — Patterns

All Aboard!

Name _____

Figure out the pattern on each train. Then fill in the missing numbers.

1. 3, 6, 9, 12, ___, ___, ___

2. 1, 11, 21, 31, ___, ___, ___

3. 20, 18, 16, 14, ___, ___, ___

4. 12, 23, 34, 45, ___, ___, ___

5. 94, 84, 74, 64, ___, ___, ___

6. 1, 2, 4, 7, ___, ___, ___

Gifted & Talented Math Grade 1 — Patterns

Caterpillar Patterns

Name _____

Study the pattern on each caterpillar. Then complete the pattern.

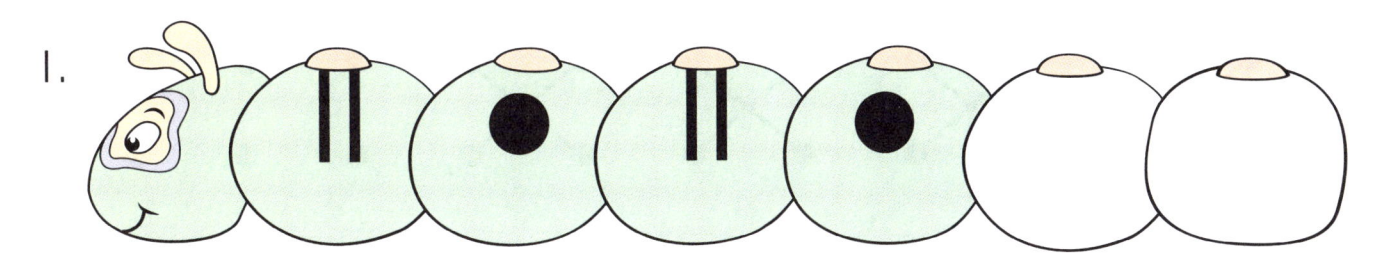

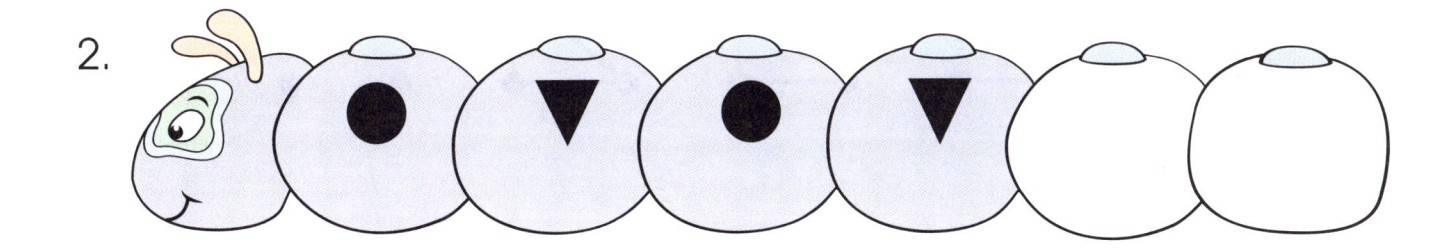

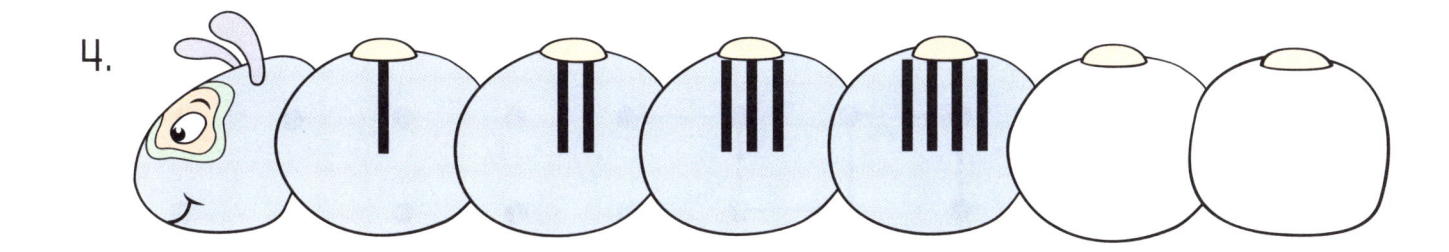

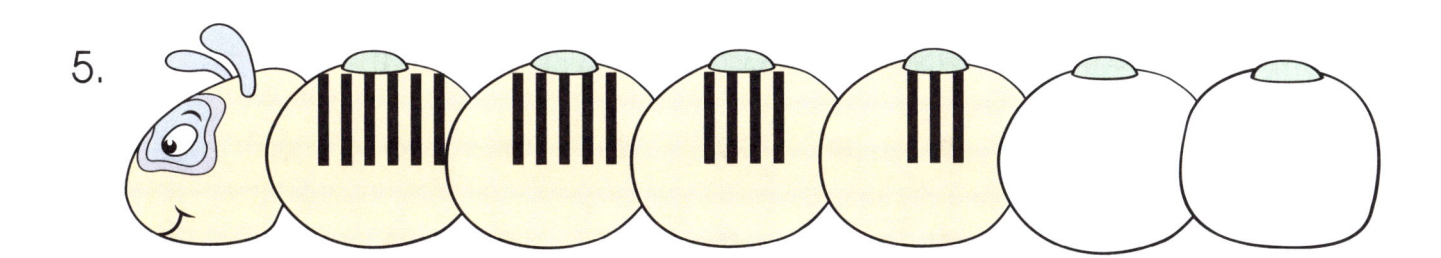

1. ‖ ● ‖ ● __ __

2. ● ▼ ● ▼ __ __

3. ● | ●● ‖ __ __

4. | ‖ ‖‖ ‖‖‖ __ __

5. ‖‖‖‖ ‖‖‖ ‖‖ ‖ __ __

Dots and Lines

Name _____

Connect the dots to extend each pattern.

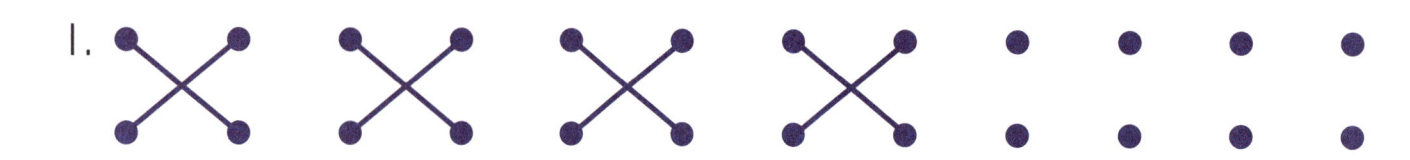

1.

2.

3.

4.

5.

Now connect the dots to make your own pattern!

Gifted & Talented Math Grade 1 24 Patterns

Shape Patterns

Name _____

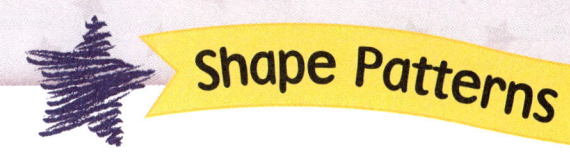

Look at each row. Draw the shape that comes next.

1.

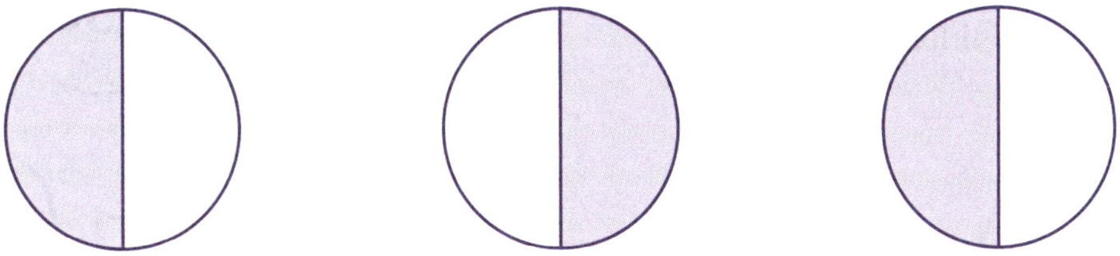

2.

3.

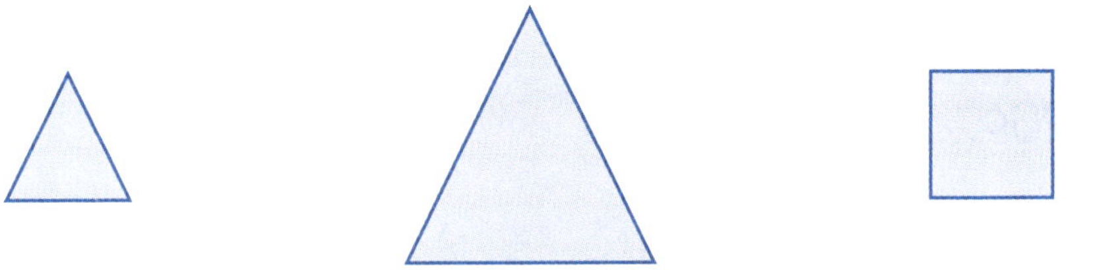

4.

5.

6.

Gifted & Talented Math Grade 1																	Patterns

Name _____

Piggy Bank Riddles

Read the clues. Draw what is in each piggy bank. Show quarters, nickels, dimes, and pennies.

1. There are two coins. They add up to 35¢.

2. There are three coins. They add up to 20¢.

3. There are three coins. They add up to 45¢.

4. There are four coins. They add up to 50¢.

5. There are five coins. They add up to 46¢.

Gifted & Talented Math Grade 1 — Money

Make 25 Cents

Name _____

Draw coins to show eight different ways you can make 25 cents.

1.	5.
2.	6.
3.	7.
4.	8.

Gifted & Talented Math Grade 1 — Money

Coin Patterns

Name _____

Solve these problems involving patterns with coins.

1. Jack had some coins. He began laying them out in a pattern like this:

   Jack used ten coins. How many cents did he have? Label the coins below, and write the amount to show your answer.

   (1¢)(10¢)( )( )( )( )( )( )( )( ) = _____ ¢

2. Lisa laid out some coins in a pattern, too. Her pattern looked like this:

   How much money did Lisa have after she laid down ten coins? Label the coins below, and write the amount to show your answer.

   (1¢)(10¢)( )( )( )( )( )( )( )( ) = _____ ¢

3. Who had more money—Jack or Lisa? _____

Gifted & Talented Math Grade 1   Money

A Toy Sale

Name _____

This sale sign was posted at a toy shop. Look at the prices of the toys. Then solve the problems.

Super Sale!

Whistle	—	5 cents
Top	—	10 cents
Car	—	15 cents
Yo-yo	—	20 cents

1. Amanda bought two different toys. She spent 20 cents. What did she buy? _____

2. Jessie bought three different toys. He spent 35 cents. What did he buy? _____

3. Carl and Lee each bought a toy. Carl's toy cost 15 cents more than Lee's toy. What did each child buy? Carl _____ Lee _____

4. Janet wants to spend exactly 25 cents. List the different sets of toys she could buy.

_____

_____

_____

Gifted & Talented Math Grade 1   Money

At the Balloon Shop

Name _____

Some children went to the balloon shop. Write the letters of the balloons they bought.

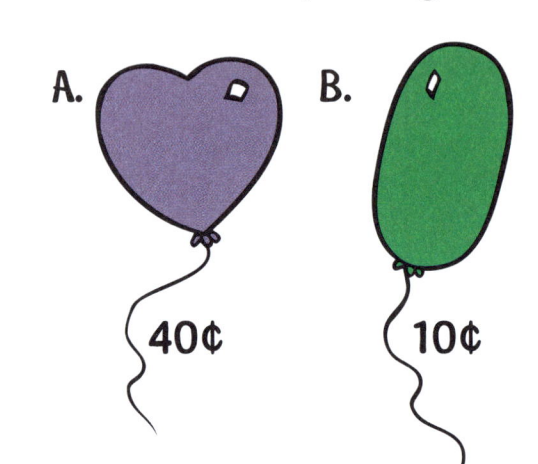

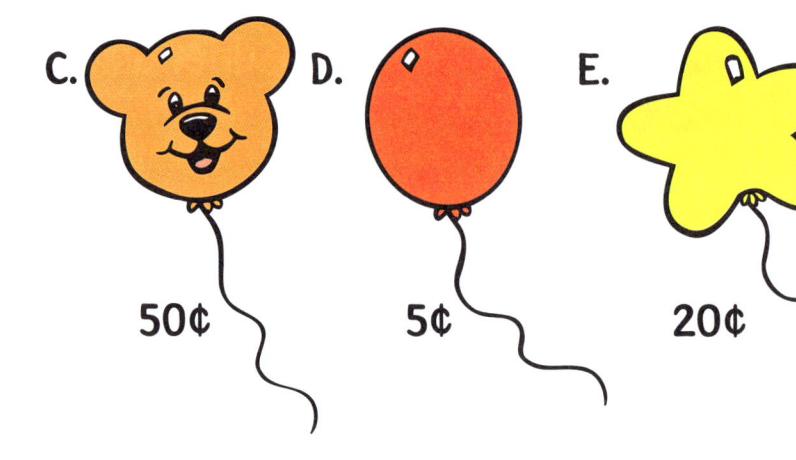

A. 40¢   B. 10¢   C. 50¢   D. 5¢   E. 20¢

1. Sam bought two balloons. He paid 30 cents. Which balloons did he buy? _____

2. Shannon bought two balloons. She paid 70 cents. Which balloons did she buy? _____

3. Mark wanted to buy two different balloons. What is the least amount of money he could have spent? _____ What is the most amount of money he could have spent? _____

4. Katie bought three different balloons. She spent 80 cents. Which balloons did she buy? _____

5. Kent bought three different balloons. He spent 65 cents. Which balloons did he buy? _____

Gifted & Talented Math Grade 1   Money

A Flower Garden

Name _____

Mrs. Potter has eight flowers in her garden. Each flower is a solid color. The flowers are red, purple, orange, or yellow.

Read the clues. Figure out how many flowers of each color Mrs. Potter has. Then color the flowers.

Clues:
- There are more yellow flowers than orange flowers.
- There are more red flowers than purple flowers.
- There are the same number of yellow and purple flowers.

Gifted & Talented Math Grade 1

Logical Thinking

Name _____

Toy Bunnies

Megan has six toy bunnies. Each one is a different color. Megan also has three baskets. She will put two bunnies in each basket.

Read the clues. Then color the pictures to show how Megan will pair the bunnies.

Clues:
- The pink bunny can go with the black bunny or the blue bunny.
- The brown bunny can go with the purple bunny or the black bunny.
- The purple bunny can go only with the yellow bunny.

Gifted & Talented Math Grade 1

Logical Thinking

Four Dinosaurs

Name _____

There are four dinosaurs standing in a line. Read the clues below. Then color the dinosaurs to show in which order they are standing.

Clues: • The green dinosaur is behind the yellow dinosaur.

• The brown dinosaur is behind the red dinosaur.

• The brown dinosaur is not the last in line.

Gifted & Talented Math Grade 1

Logical Thinking

Four Brothers

Name _____

Ted, Ed, Fred, and Jed are brothers. Use the clues to find out which boy is the shortest, which boy is the tallest, and which boys are in-between. Then write their names under their pictures.

Clues:
- Ed is taller than Fred.
- Ted is taller than Jed.
- Fred is taller than Ted.

_____   _____   _____   _____

Gifted & Talented Math Grade 1

Logical Thinking

Taking a Trip

Name _____

The Lang family is going on a trip. Read the clues to find out where the family members sit in the van. Then write their names on the correct seat.

Clues: • One parent drives.

• Matt, the youngest, sits behind his mom.

• Ruff, the family's dog, sits in the back.

• Anna sits behind the driver.

• Eric sits behind his little brother.

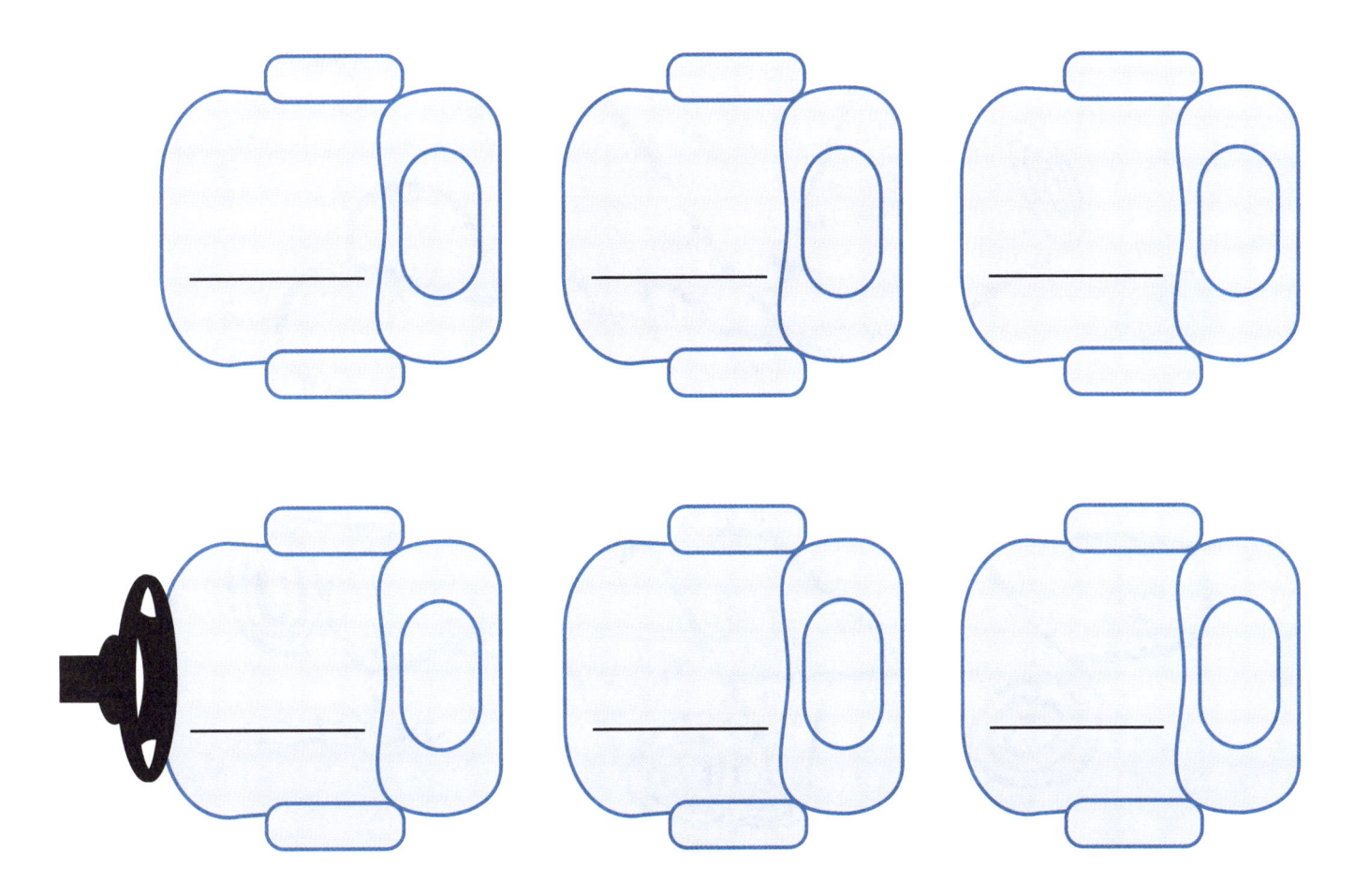

Gifted & Talented Math Grade 1   Logical Thinking

Eager Beaver

Name _____

Eager Beaver has gathered a pile of sticks to begin building his lodge. Now he has changed his mind, and he wants to move his lodge somewhere else! Eager Beaver must move one stick at a time. He cannot move any stick that is covered by another stick. Look at the picture below. Number the sticks from 1 to 6 to show the order Eager Beaver must move them.

Gifted & Talented Math Grade 1

Logical Thinking

Sorting Shapes

Name _____

Miss Baker asked her class to sort eight shapes into two groups. Look at how Randy and Sandy sorted the shapes. Then label each group.

Randy's Groups

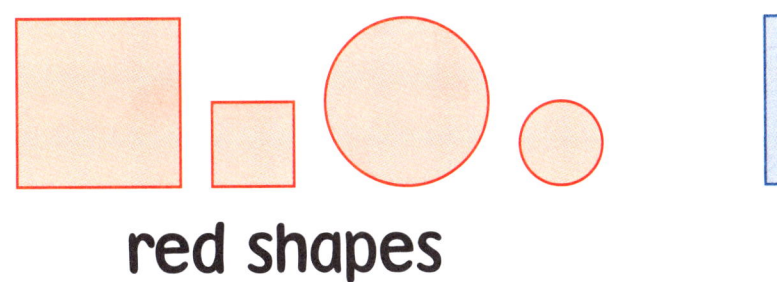

red shapes   _____

Sandy's Groups

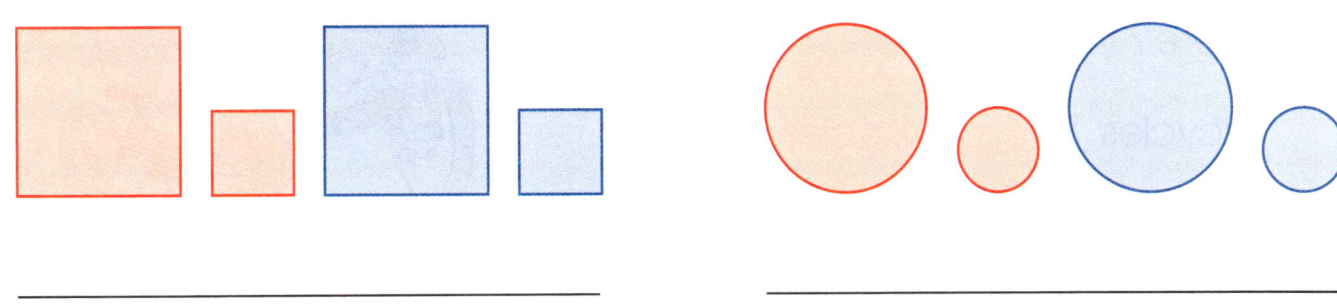

_____   _____

Draw two other groups you could make with the shapes. Label your groups.

_____   _____

Circus Fun

Name _____

Here comes the circus parade! Read these problems and solve them.

1. Kristen was watching the clowns and horses in the parade. She counted 7 heads and 20 legs. How many clowns and horses did she see?

   clowns _____ horses _____

2. Some clowns in the parade were riding bicycles. Other clowns were riding tricycles. There were 12 wheels in all. How many bicycles and tricycles were there?

   bicycles _____ tricycles _____

3. One clown was holding red and blue balloons. The clown had 15 balloons altogether. There were twice as many red balloons as there were blue balloons. How many balloons were red and how many were blue?

   red balloons _____ blue balloons _____

Gifted & Talented Math Grade 1   Logical Thinking

Which Clown?

Name _____

Read each set of clues. Write the letter of the clown that is being described.

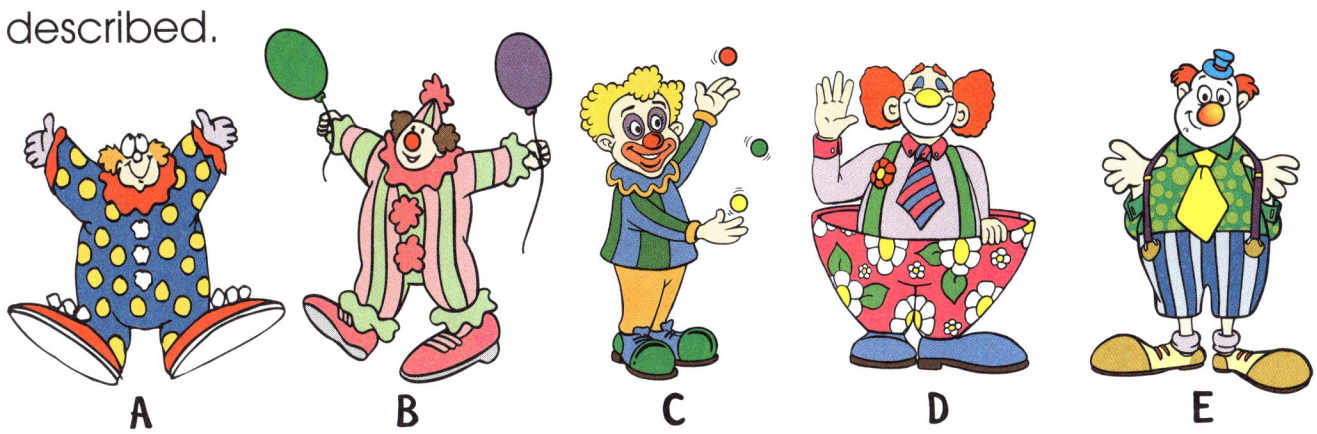

A   B   C   D   E

1. He has a hat.
   He has suspenders.
   He has dots.

   _____

2. He has suspenders.
   He has no hat.
   He has a necktie.

   _____

3. He has no hat.
   He has dots.
   He has no necktie.

   _____

4. He has no necktie.
   He has stripes.
   He has a hat.

   _____

Which clown is not described above? _____ Write three clues about him.

_____

_____

_____

_____

Gifted & Talented Math Grade 1   39   Logical Thinking

Roger's Triangles

Name _____

Roger has made some special triangles. Study the numbers on the triangles carefully. Then fill in the missing numbers.

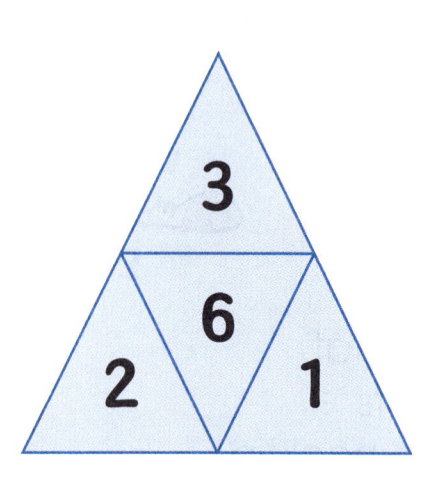

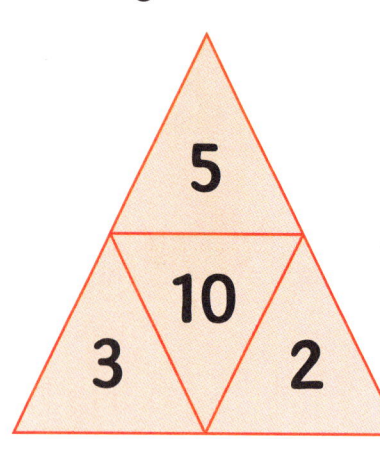

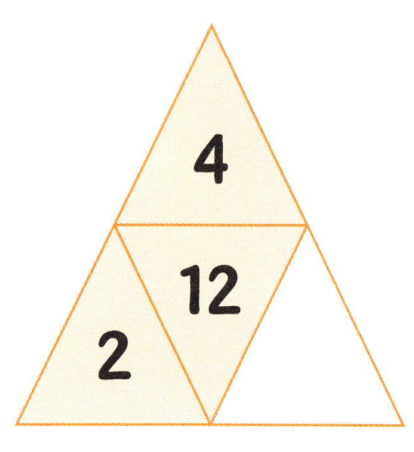

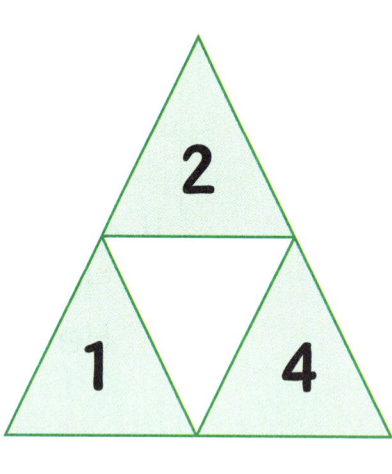

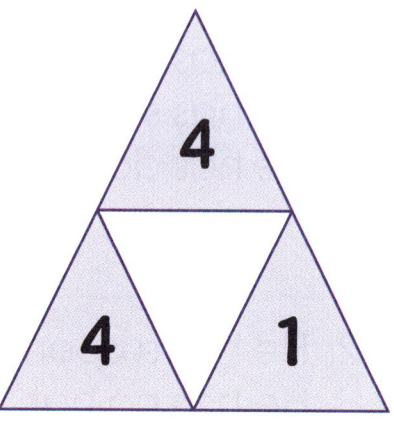

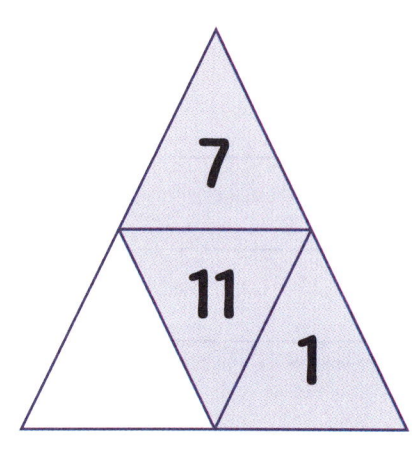

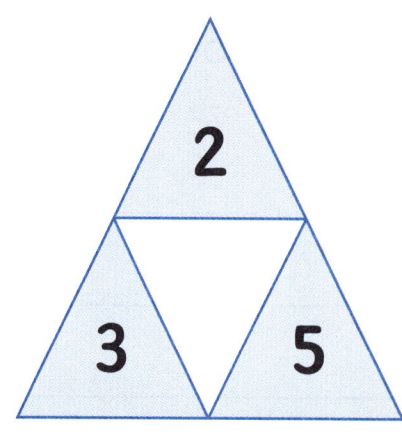

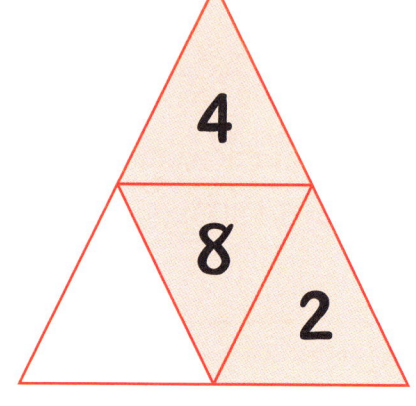

Gifted & Talented Math Grade 1 — Logical Thinking

How Many Cookies?

Name _____

Mrs. Lee made some cookies for her friends. She put the cookies in round boxes and square boxes. All the round boxes had the same number of cookies. All the square boxes had the same number of cookies.

Study the pictures. Figure out how many cookies were in each box.

🔵 + 🟥 = 16 cookies

🔵 + 🔵 + 🟥 = 22 cookies

🟥 + 🟥 + 🔵 = 26 cookies

How many cookies were in the 🔵 ? _____

How many cookies were in the 🟥 ? _____

Gifted & Talented Math Grade 1 — 41 — Logical Thinking

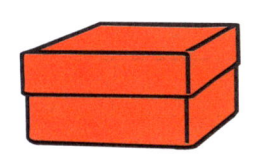

Library Lineup

Eight children are waiting for the library to open. Look at the lineup and solve the problems.

1. Sue is fifth in line. How many children are behind Sue? _____

2. Matt is third in line. How many children are behind Matt? _____

3. Eric is sixth in line. How many children are before him? _____

4. Jill is fourth in line. Amy is eighth in line. How many children are between Jill and Amy? _____

5. Lee is second in line. Toby is seventh in line. How many children are between Lee and Toby? _____

6. Dan is first in line. How many children are between him and the last boy in line? _____

7. Write the names of the children in the order they are lined up. Begin with the first child and end with the last.

_____

_____

Gifted & Talented Math Grade 1   Logical Thinking

To the Doghouse

Name _____

Guess the length of each path in inches. Write your guess in the box labeled **My Guess**. Then check your guess by measuring the path with a ruler. Write the actual length in the box labeled **My Check**.

_____
one inch

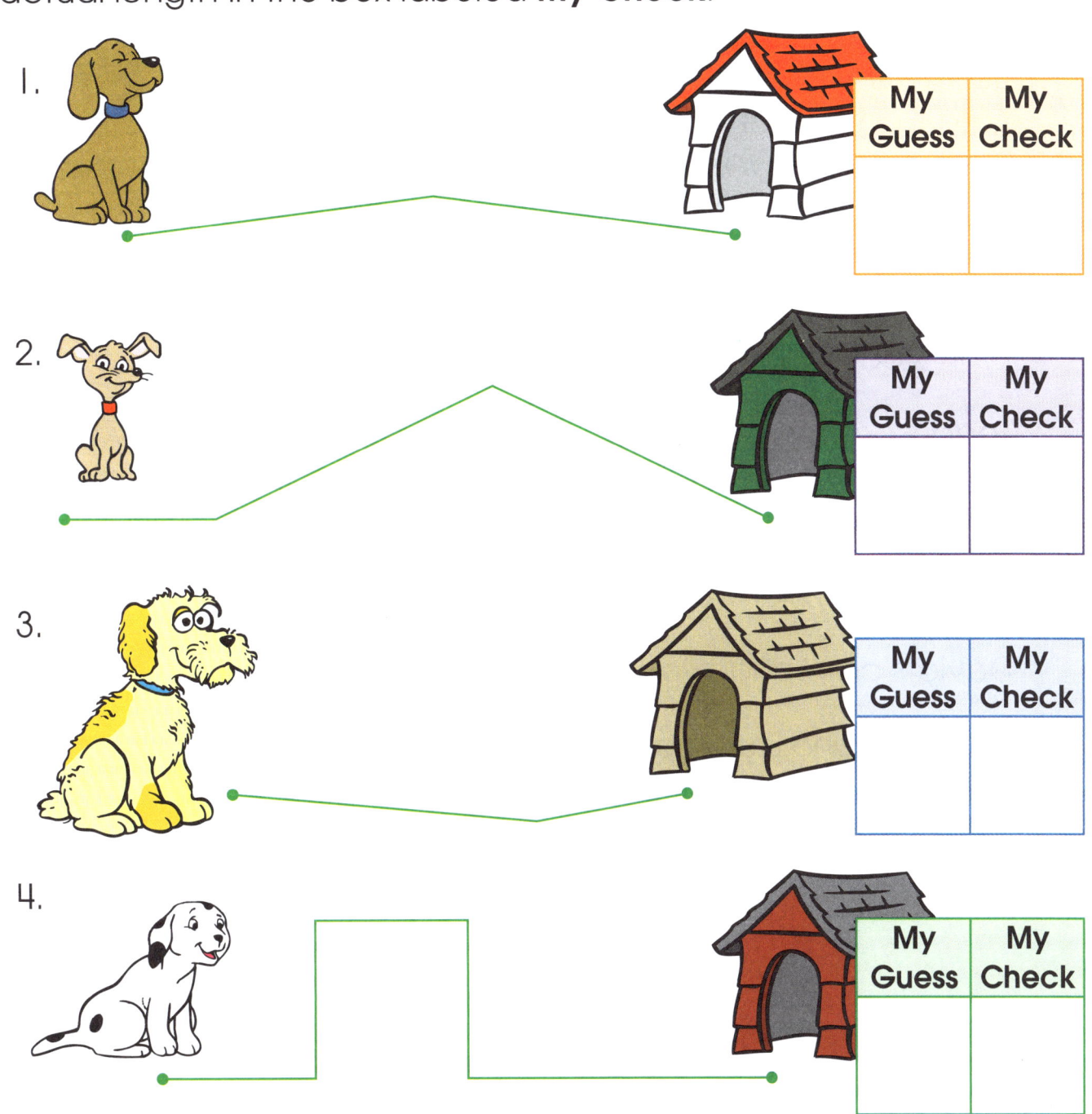

1.

My Guess	My Check

2.

My Guess	My Check

3.

My Guess	My Check

4.

My Guess	My Check

Gifted & Talented Math Grade 1

Measurement

Paper Caterpillars

Name _____

Mr. Parker's class glued paper circles together to make caterpillars. Solve the following problems to find out how long some of the caterpillars were.

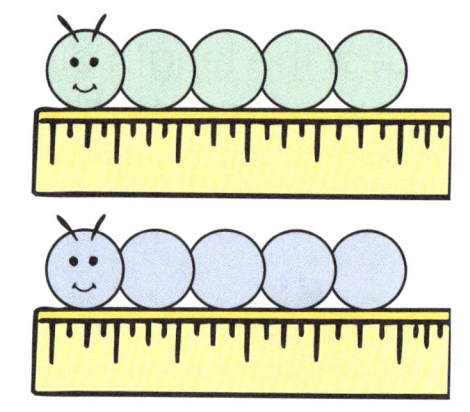

1. Ben's caterpillar was 8 inches long. Kate's caterpillar was 2 inches shorter. Lynn's caterpillar was 3 inches longer than Kate's caterpillar. How long were Kate's and Lynn's caterpillars?

   Kate's caterpillar was _____ inches long.

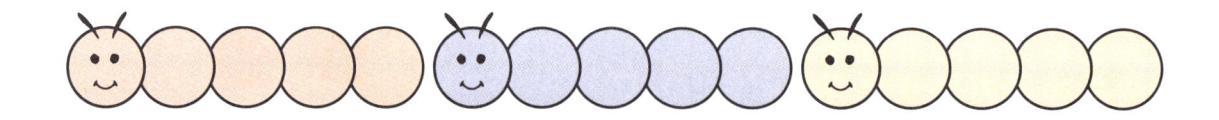

   Lynn's caterpillar was _____ inches long.

2. Todd's caterpillar was 7 inches long. Rick's caterpillar was 3 inches longer than Todd's. Rick's caterpillar was twice as long as David's. How long were Rick's and David's caterpillars?

   Rick's caterpillar was _____ inches long.

   David's caterpillar was _____ inches long.

3. Ann, Jan, and Fran made caterpillars that were the same length. The girls placed the caterpillars in a line. The line measured 18 inches. How long was each caterpillar?

   Each caterpillar was _____ inches long.

Name _____

Heavier or Lighter?

Look at each pair of items. Circle the one that is heavier or lighter.

1. Which is heavier?

    balloon   basketball

2. Which is lighter?

    feather   cup

3. Which is heavier?

    bowl   pencil

4. Which is lighter?

    spoon   straw

Draw something that is lighter than an apple. Draw something that is heavier than an apple.

| lighter than an apple | | heavier than an apple |

Gifted & Talented Math Grade 1   Measurement

Ounces or Pounds?

Name _____

A fork weighs about one ounce.

A shoe weighs about one pound.

Write ounces or pounds to show how much each object weighs. Write the word that makes the most sense.

1.  about 4 _____

2.  about 10 _____

3.  about 8 _____

4.  about 15 _____

5.  about 2 _____

6.  about 2 _____

Gifted & Talented Math Grade 1 — Measurement

Name _____

How Much Time Does It Take?

How long would it take to do each activity? Circle the best answer.

1. A child eats a sandwich.

   minutes

   hours

   days

2. A seed grows into a plant.

   minutes

   hours

   days

3. A plane flies across the country.

   minutes

   hours

   days

4. People watch a baseball game.

   minutes

   hours

   days

5. A child builds a block tower.

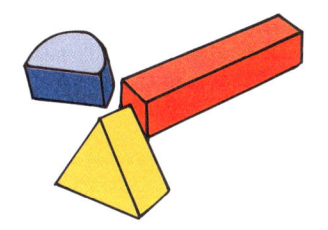

   minutes

   hours

   days

6. Workers build a house.

   minutes

   hours

   days

What is one thing that takes you only a few minutes to do?

_____

What is one thing that takes you over an hour to do?

_____

Gifted & Talented Math Grade 1   47   Measurement

Shape Puzzles

Name _____

Each shape inside the box can be made by putting together two shapes that are outside the box. Draw a line from each shape inside the box to the two shapes that can be joined together to make it.

Gifted & Talented Math Grade 1   48   Geometry

Shape Designs

Name _____

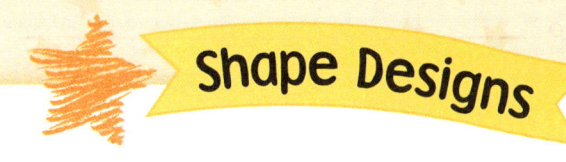

These children are describing their designs. Write the letters of the matching pictures on the correct lines.

1.  I drew three squares. None of the squares are the same size. _____

2.  I drew three different shapes. None of the shapes touch each other. _____

3.  I drew four triangles that are the same size. I drew two squares that are different sizes. _____

4.  I drew four triangles. The triangles are different sizes. _____

5.  I drew three squares. One square touches the other two squares. _____

6.  I drew three shapes. All three shapes touch one another. _____

A   B    C

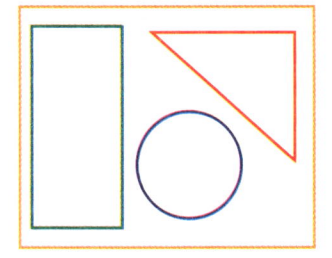

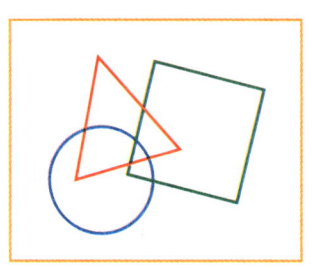

D 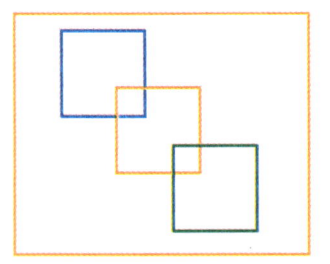   E 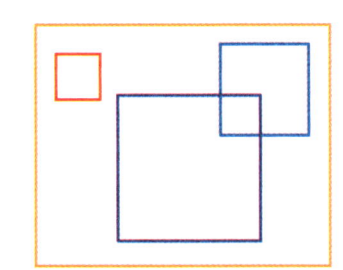   F

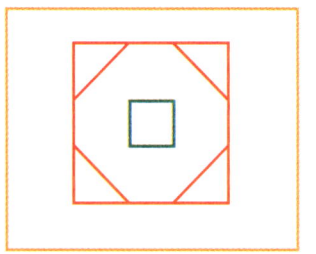

Gifted & Talented Math Grade 1   49   Geometry

Hidden Squares

Name _____

Count the total number of squares in each picture. Watch out for hidden squares!

1.

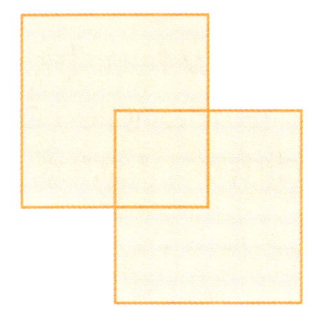

_____ squares

2.

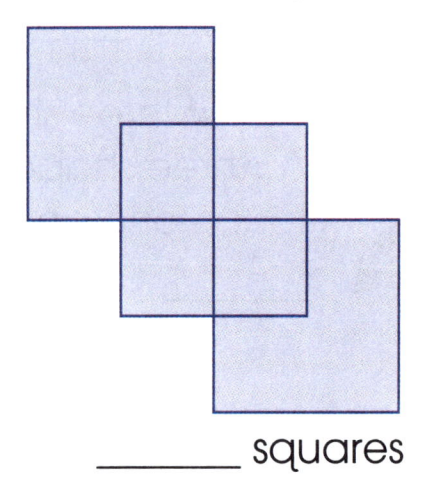

_____ squares

3.

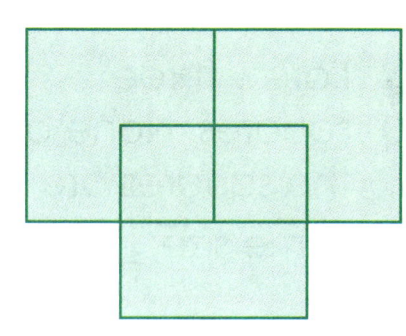

_____ squares

4.

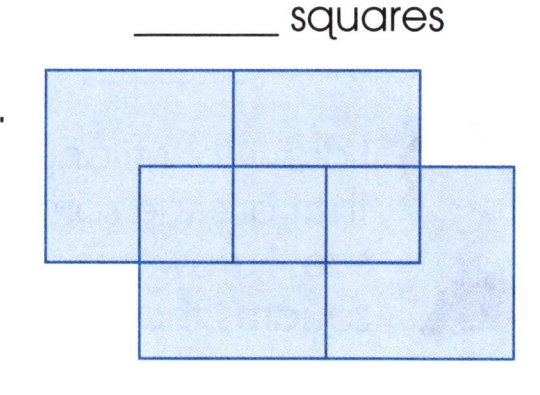

_____ squares

Draw a picture that has hidden squares.

Gifted & Talented Math Grade 1 — 50 — Geometry

How Many Triangles?

Name _____

Write how many triangles can be found in each picture.

1.

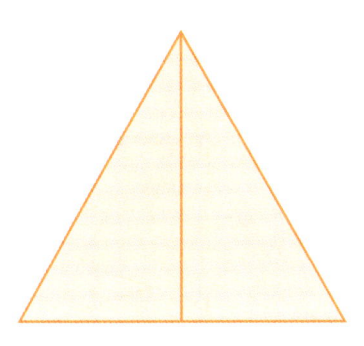

_____ triangles

2.

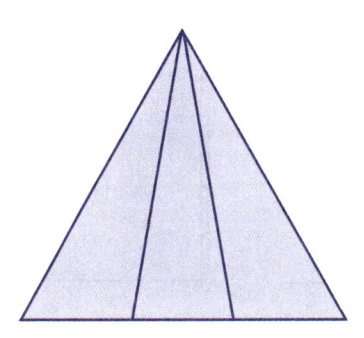

_____ triangles

3.

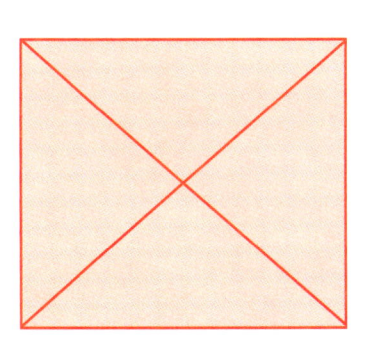

_____ triangles

4.

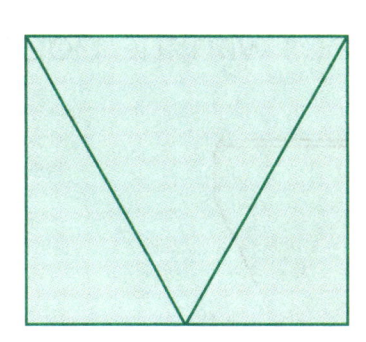

_____ triangles

5.

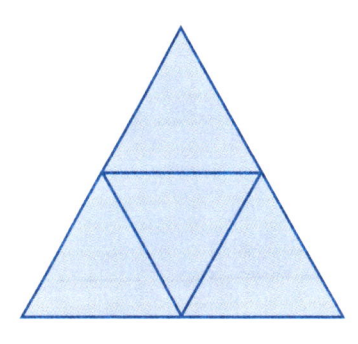

_____ triangles

6.

_____ triangles

Gifted & Talented Math Grade 1   51   Geometry

Paper Cutouts

Look at the six pieces of paper. They were folded in half and a shape was cut out of each one. Write the letters A to E to match the shapes with the paper they were cut from.

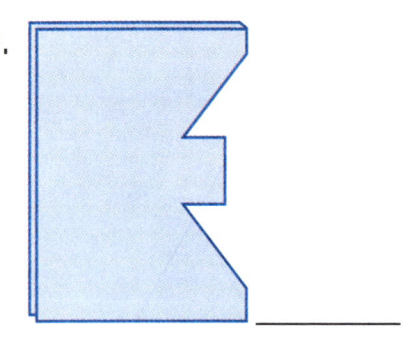

1. 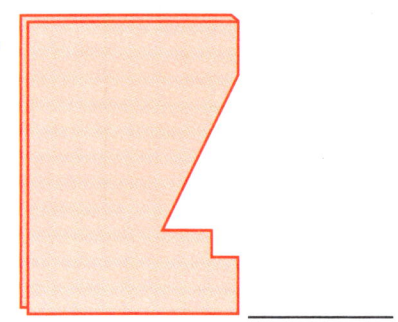 ____
2.  ____
3. 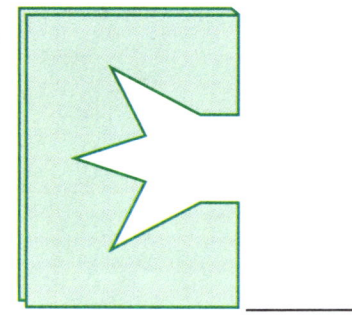 ____
4. ____
5.  ____
6. ____

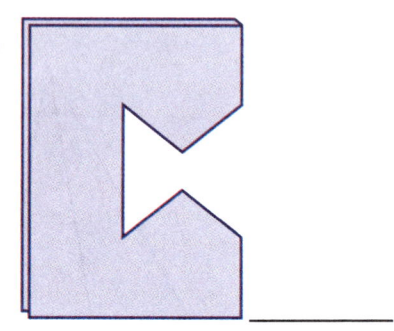

A 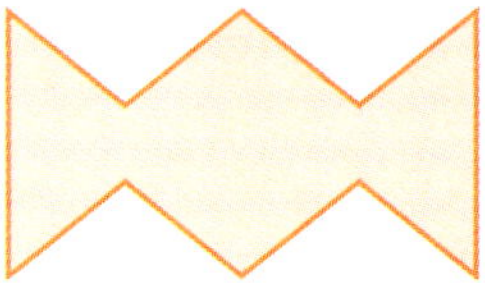
B 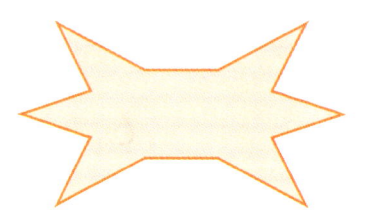
C 
D 
E 
F

Shape Search

Name _____

Look at the shape in each row. Find it in the design and color it.

1.

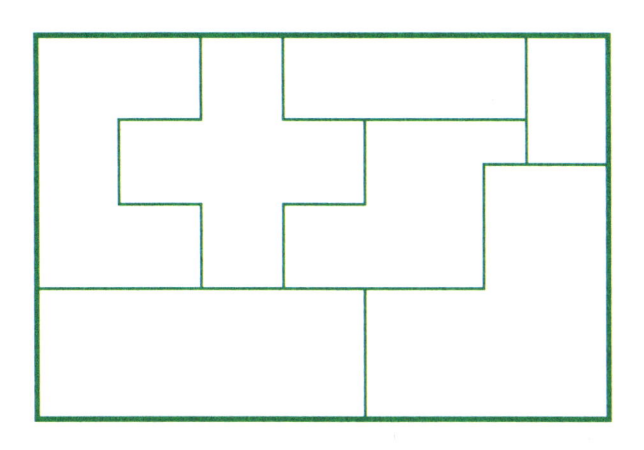

2.

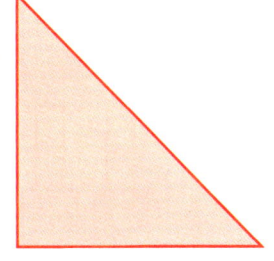

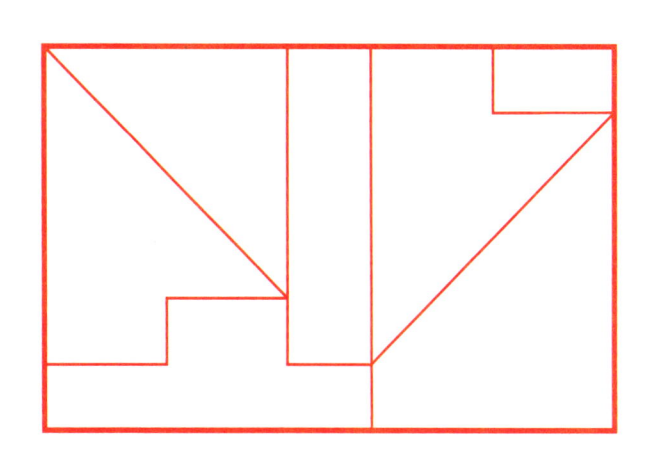

3.

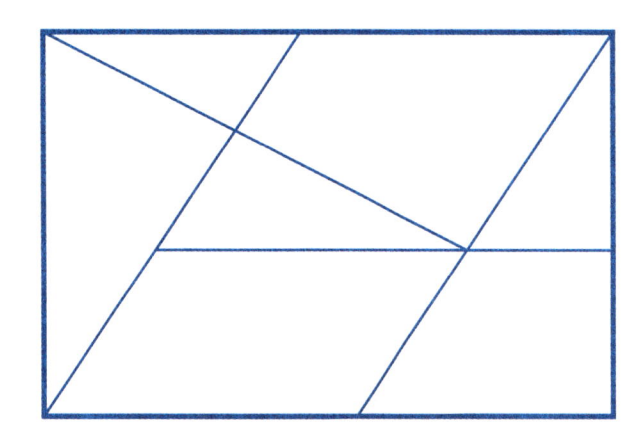

Gifted & Talented Math Grade 1 — Geometry

Robot Riddles

Name _____

Read the riddles. Write the letters of the robots they describe.

1. I have a square head. The rest of me is made of squares or rectangles. _____

2. I have a head shaped like a rectangle. I have five circles on my body. _____

3. My feet are shaped like squares. The rest of me has squares, rectangles, and triangles. _____

4. I have hands and feet made of triangles. I have two circles for each leg. _____

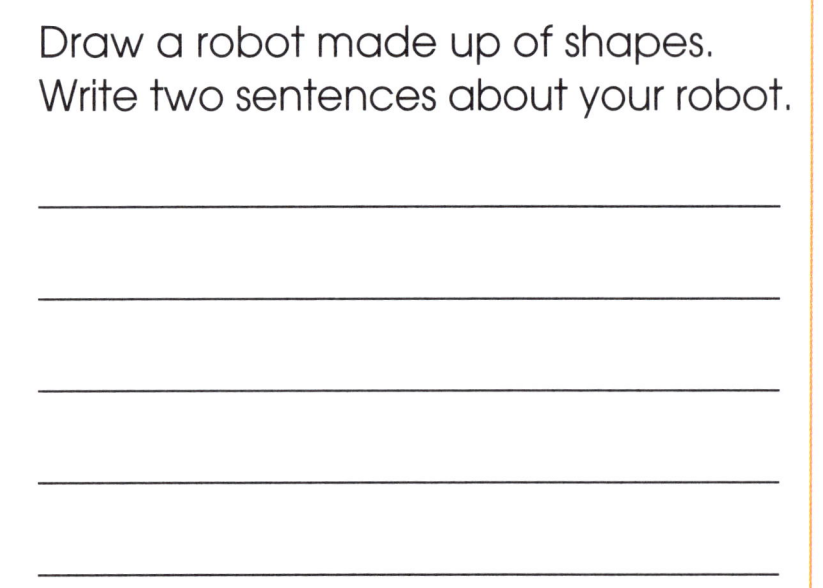

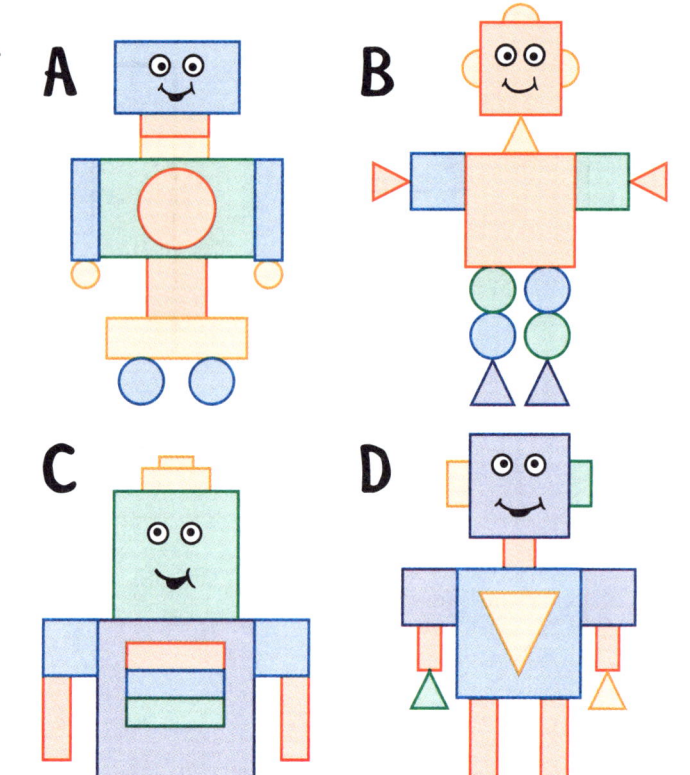

Draw a robot made up of shapes. Write two sentences about your robot.

_____
_____
_____
_____

Gifted & Talented Math Grade 1   Geometry

What's on the Bottom?

Name _____

Suppose you picked up each object below. What would its base (the bottom part) look like? Write the letter of the matching shape. (You may choose a shape more than once.)

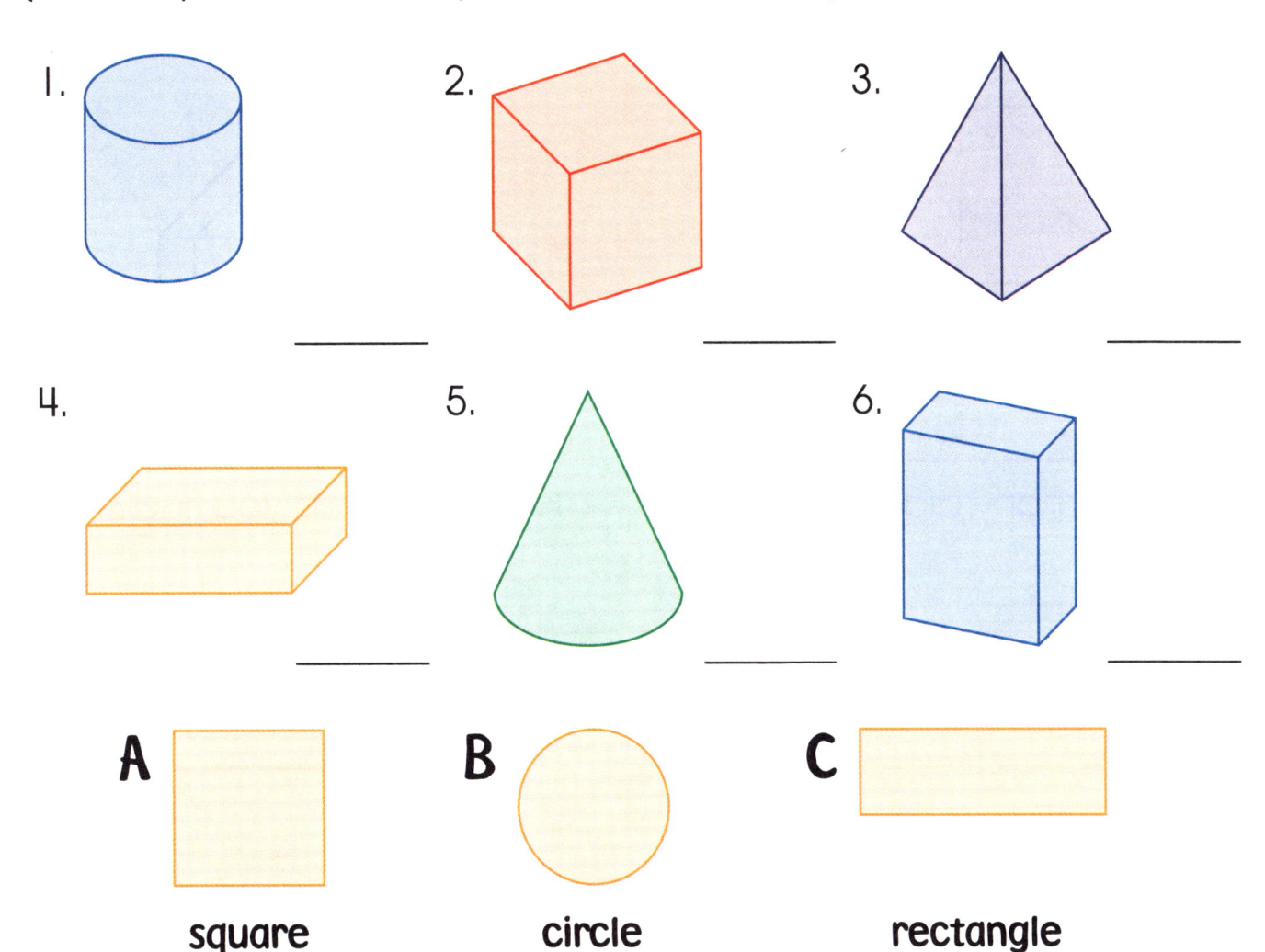

1. _____

2. _____

3. _____

4. _____

5. _____

6. _____

A — square

B — circle

C — rectangle

Look around your home. Find an object with a base shaped like a square. Find an object with a base shaped like a circle. Find an object with a base shaped like a rectangle. List the objects you find.

_____

_____

Gifted & Talented Math Grade 1 — Geometry

Color and Count

Name _____

Find the shapes. Color them. Then write how many shapes you found.

1. Color each △ .

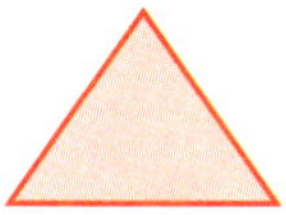

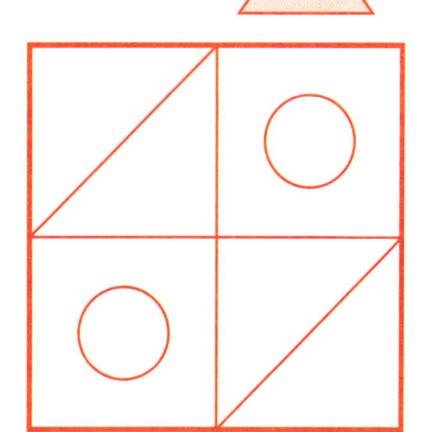

   How many did you find?
   _____

2. Color each ▱ .

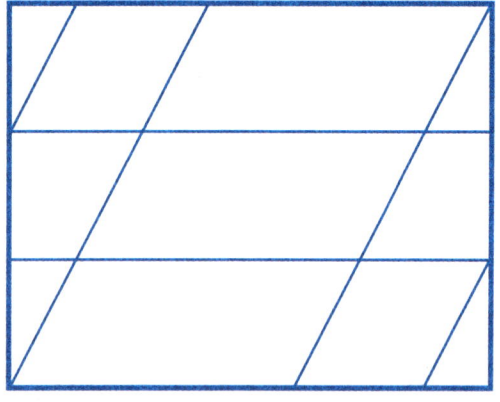

   How many did you find?
   _____

3. Color each ▢ .

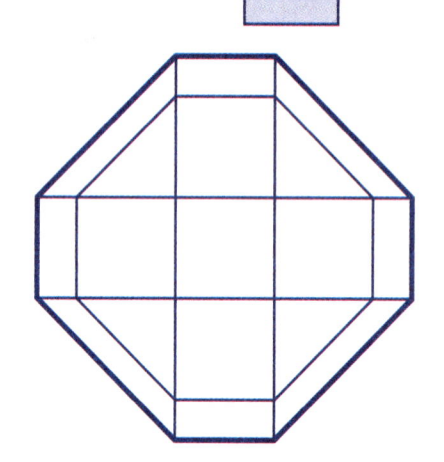

   How many did you find?
   _____

4. Color each ⏢ .

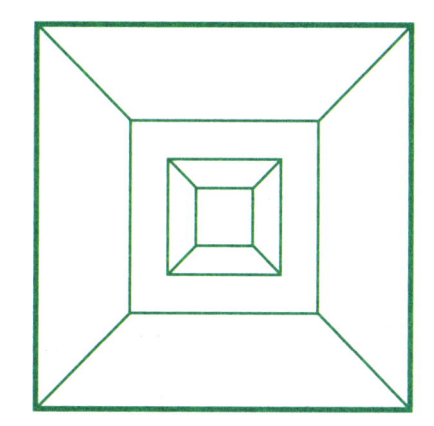

   How many did you find?
   _____

Gifted & Talented Math Grade 1 — Geometry

Cool Scoops

Name _____

Joe's ice cream shop is having a very special sale. Two scoops of ice cream are being sold for the price of one! Joe has sold so much ice cream that he has only three flavors left—chocolate, banana, and cherry.

Color the ice cream scoops brown, yellow, and red to show the different ways Joe can combine the ice cream flavors. (Joe can sell two scoops of one flavor or two scoops of two different flavors.)

Gifted & Talented Math Grade 1 — Statistics and Probability

Benny's Outfits

Name _____

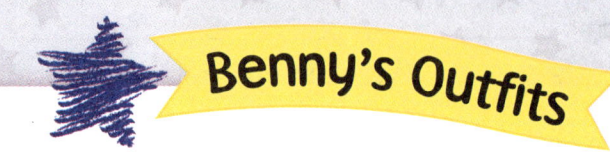

Benny has three shirts. They are green, purple, and red. Benny has three pairs of pants. They are blue, black, and brown. Color the pictures to show how many different outfits Benny can wear.

Gifted & Talented Math Grade 1 — 58 — Statistics and Probability

Jenny's Outfits

Name _____

Jenny's favorite colors are red and yellow. She has a red hat, a red T-shirt, and a red pair of shorts. She also has a yellow hat, a yellow T-shirt, and a yellow pair of shorts. Color the pictures to show how many different ways Jenny can mix and match her clothes.

Gifted & Talented Math Grade 1 — Statistics and Probability

Goldfish Pets

Name _____

Meg   Greg   Sue   Dru

Color the graph to show how many pets each child has. Then answer the questions.

Number of Goldfish

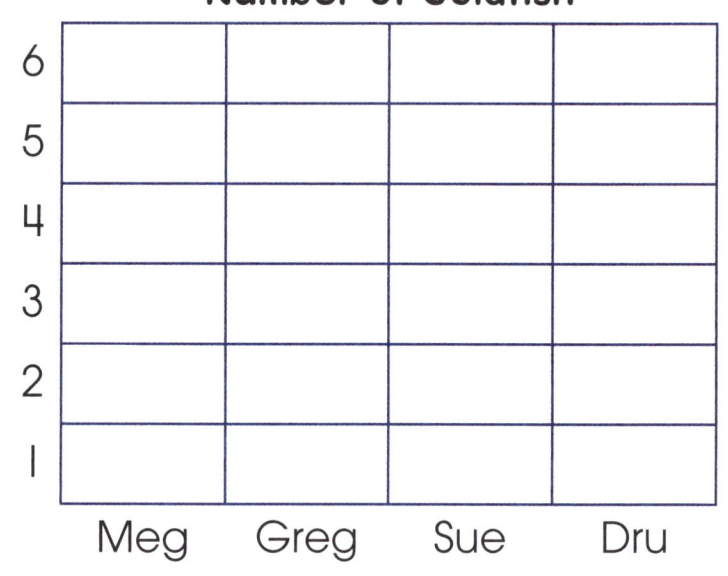

	Meg	Greg	Sue	Dru
6				
5				
4				
3				
2				
1				

1. Who has the most goldfish? _____

2. Who has the fewest goldfish? _____

3. Who has half as many fish as Dru? _____

4. Who has three more fish than Meg? _____

5. How many fish do the four children have altogether? _____

Gifted & Talented Math Grade 1   Statistics and Probability

Answers

Page 5
Numbers left in the box: 6, 14, 18

Page 6

Page 7

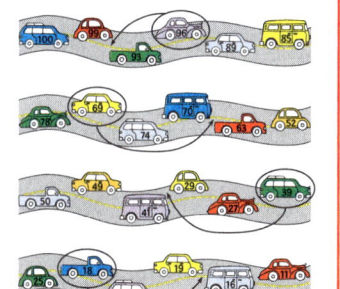

Page 8
1. Eric
2. Joni
3. Abby
4. Ryan
5. Todd
6. Becky

Page 9

Numbers should be written as follows: 2, 4, 6, 8, 10, 12, 14, 16, 18, 20, 22, 24, 26.

Page 10

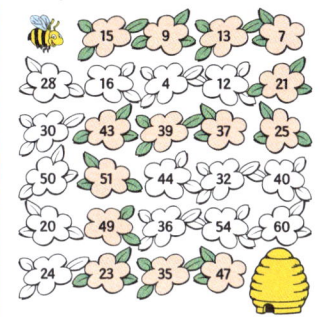

Page 11
1. 32
2. 57
3. 64
4. 27
5. 86
6. 79
7. 82

Pages 12 and 13
1. 11
2. 18
3. 60
4. 35

Clues and mystery number will vary.

Page 14
1. 5
2. 6
3. 7
4. 6
5. 10
6. 9

Page 15
1. 6 + 3 = 11 − 2
2. 5 − 2 = 10 − 7
3. 6 + 2 = 12 − 4
4. 8 + 6 = 9 + 5
5. 12 − 3 = 17 − 8
6. 16 − 8 = 5 + 3
7. 9 + 6 = 8 + 7
8. 11 − 3 = 17 − 9

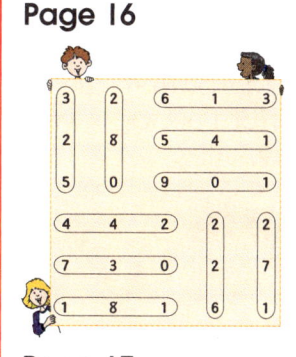

Page 16

Page 17
Answers will vary. Here are some examples:
1 + 2 + 9 = 12
2 + 4 + 6 = 12
3 + 4 + 5 = 12
2 + 3 + 7 = 12
1 + 2 + 3 + 6 = 12
1 + 2 + 4 + 5 = 12

Page 18
(One way your child might solve the problem is by manipulating pieces of paper that have been numbered 1 to 9. Suggest starting with the numbers that add up to 7—1, 2, 4. Then let your child rearrange the remaining six numbers to figure out the answers for 15 and 23.)

15—3, 5, 7; 7—1, 2, 4; 23—6, 8, 9

Page 19
Balloons should be completed as follows: 1, 6, 8; 4, 2, 9; 5, 7, 3.

Page 20
(If you wish, give your child pieces of colored paper or other objects to work out the problems. In the first problem, your child can take eight pieces of paper and divide them into two equal groups. In the second problem, your child can lay down one piece of red paper and two pieces of yellow paper; your child should keep doing this until he or she gets 12 pieces of paper. In the third problem, your child

can arrange eight pieces of paper into two groups so that one group has four more pieces than the other.)
1. boys—4; girls—4
2. red balloons—4; yellow balloons—8
3. boxes—6; bags—2

Page 21
1. Frankie will land on 10. (He jumps two numbers at a time.)
2. Frankie will land on 12. (He jumps four numbers at a time.)
3. Frankie will land on 9. (He jumps one number, two numbers, one number, two numbers, and so on.)
4. Frankie will land on 10. (He jumps one number, two numbers, three numbers, four numbers.)

Page 22
1. 15, 18 (Add 3.)
2. 41, 51 (Add 10.)
3. 12, 10 (Subtract 2.)
4. 56, 67 (Add 11.)
5. 54, 44 (Subtract 10.)
6. 11, 16 (Add 1, add 2, add 3, and so on.)

Page 23
Caterpillars should be completed as follows:
1. two lines, one dot
2. dot, triangle
3. three dots, three lines
4. five lines, six lines
5. two lines, one line

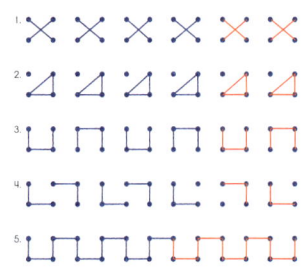

Page 24
Child's pattern at bottom of page will vary.

Page 25

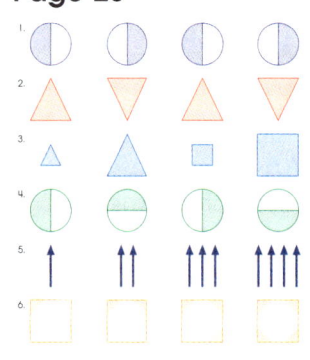

Page 26

Page 27
Coin combinations will vary. There are 13 possible combinations.
1 quarter
2 dimes, 1 nickel
2 dimes, 5 pennies
1 dime, 3 nickels
1 dime, 2 nickels, 5 pennies
1 dime, 1 nickel, 10 pennies
1 dime, 15 pennies
5 nickels
4 nickels, 5 pennies
3 nickels, 10 pennies
2 nickels, 15 pennies
1 nickel, 20 pennies
25 pennies

Page 28
(Your child may wish to lay out real coins to solve these problems.)
1. Coin amounts should be filled out (1¢, 10¢, 1¢, 10¢, and so on). Jack—55¢
2. Coin amounts should be filled out 95¢, 10¢, 1¢, 5¢, 10¢, 1¢, and so on). Lisa—53¢
3. Jack

Page 29
1. whistle, car
2. yo-yo, car
3. Carl—yo-yo; Lee—whistle

4. 5 whistles; 2 tops and 1 whistle; 1 car and 1 top; 1 car and 2 whistles; 1 yo-yo and 1 whistle

Page 30
1. B, E
2. C, E
3. least amount—15¢; most amount—90¢
4. B, C, E
5. A, D, E

Page 31
Flowers should be colored as follows: 3 red, 2 yellow, 2 purple, 1 orange.

Page 32
(Your child should begin this problem by pairing the purple and yellow bunnies since this is the only possible color combination involving the purple.) The bunnies should be colored as follows: purple and yellow; brown and black; pink and blue.

Page 33
(Your child may want to manipulate red, green, yellow, and brown paper squares to solve the problem.)

The dinosaurs should be colored as follows (from left to right): red, brown, yellow, green.

Page 34
From shortest to tallest—Jed, Ted, Fred, Ed

Page 35

Page 36

Page 37
Randy's Groups—red shapes, blue shapes
Sandy's Groups—squares, circles
Shapes can be drawn and labeled to show one group with big shapes and the other group with little shapes.

Page 38
One way your child can solve these problems is by reading the information and making a guess. Then based on the criteria, your child revise his or her guess. For example, suppose your child guesses 3 clowns and 4 horses in the first problem. He or she will determine that though the number of heads is correct, the number of legs is too high; your child will then need to adjust the original guess.
1. clowns—4; horses—3
2. bicycles—3; tricycles—2
3. red balloons—10; blue balloons—5

Page 39
1. E
2. D
3. A
4. B

C is not described. Suggestions for clues: He has no hat. He has stripes. He has no suspenders.

Page 40

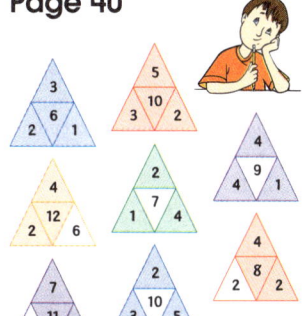

Page 41
round box—6
square box—10

Page 42
1. 3
2. 5
3. 5
4. 3
5. 4
6. 5
7. Dan, Lee, Matt, Jill, Sue, Eric, Toby, Amy

Page 43
Guesses will vary. Actual lengths in inches are as follows:
1. 4
2. 5
3. 3
4. 6

Page 44
1. Kate's caterpillar—6 inches; Lynn's caterpillar—9 inches
2. Rick's caterpillar—10 inches; David's caterpillar—5 inches
3. Each caterpillar was 6 inches long.

Page 45
These pictures should be circled:
1. basketball
2. feather
3. bowl
4. straw
Drawings will vary.

Page 46
1. ounces
2. pounds
3. ounces
4. pounds
5. ounces
6. pounds

Page 47
1. minutes
2. days
3. hours
4. hours
5. minutes
6. days

Answers to questions will vary.

Page 48

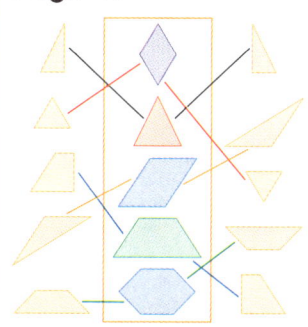

Page 49
1. E
2. A
3. F
4. B
5. D
6. C

Page 50
1. 3
2. 7
3. 5
4. 7

Page 51
1. 3 triangles
2. 6 triangles (3 small triangles, 2 formed by two triangles, one formed by three triangles)
3. 8 triangles (4 small triangles, 4 formed by two triangles)
4. 3 triangles
5. 5 triangles (4 small triangles, 1 formed by four triangles)
6. 12 triangles (6 small triangles, 2 triangles formed by two triangles, 4 triangles formed by three triangles)

Page 52
1. E
2. F
3. B
4. C
5. D
6. A

Page 53

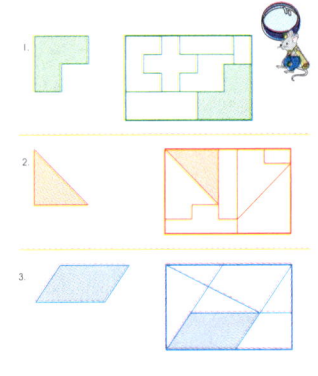

Page 54
1. C
2. A
3. D
4. B

Picture and sentences will vary.

Page 55
1. B
2. A
3. A
4. C
5. B
6. C

List of objects will vary.

Page 56
1. 4
2. 5
3. 5
4. 8

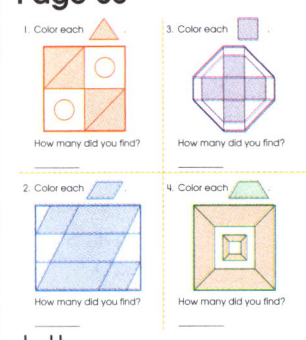

Page 57
Ice cream scoops should be colored with these six pairs of colors: brown/brown; yellow/yellow; red/red; brown/yellow; brown/red; yellow/red.

Page 58
T-shirts/pants should be colored with these nine pairs of colors:
green/blue; green/black; green/brown
purple/blue; purple/black; purple/brown
red/blue; red/black; red/brown

Page 59
T-shirt/shorts/hat should be colored with these eight combinations of colors:
red/red/red; red/red/yellow; red/yellow/red; red/yellow/yellow
yellow/yellow/yellow; yellow/yellow/red; yellow/red/yellow; yellow/red/red

Page 60
1. Dru
2. Meg
3. Sue
4. Greg
5. 16